NEEDLEWORK
MASTERPIECES
~ *from* ~
WINTERTHUR

NEEDLEWORK
MASTERPIECES
~ *from* ~
# WINTERTHUR

HOLLIS GREER MINOR

David & Charles

CADCC

A DAVID & CHARLES BOOK

First published in the UK in 1998

ISBN 0 7153 0705 3

Photography by Tim Hill
Styling by Zöe Hill
Book design by Maggie Aldred
Printed in Singapore by C. S. Graphics Pte Ltd
for David & Charles
Brunel House   Newton Abbot   Devon

25⁹⁵

CONTENTS

INTRODUCTION

This book contains some of my favourite patterns adapted from the exquisite decorative arts collection of Winterthur Museum, Garden and Library in Delaware, USA. The sumptuous photography and vibrant full-colour charts will enable you to make cushions, pictures, purses and more, all adapted from timeless historical designs. The story behind each pattern is also provided to give you a better understanding of the role that design and technique have played throughout the ages.

Learn how to use the charts for three of today's most popular needlework methods: needlepoint, multi-stitch canvas work and counted cross-stitch, and find out how to use lovely multi-fibres and alter colourways to fit your personal taste. This enables you to use the same charts for hundreds of projects, in different needlework styles and colours, making this book an invaluable resource for years to come.

This book is an outgrowth of my career in needlework design which began almost three decades ago when I started painting one-of-a-kind custom needlepoint canvases and charting cross-stitch patterns for individuals and shops. After almost 10 years, my needlework design ability of seeing everything in terms of tiny dots of colour, pieced together to match the spirit of an original piece, delighted museum personnel, and it became my career.

I started It's Polite to Point® in 1979, to produce needlework products exclusively for cultural and conservation organizations, which receive a portion of the proceeds. Now the company supplies affordable, heirloom-quality museum adaptations internationally to catalogues as well as fine needlework, museum, gift and department stores. I also developed a line of fine-quality needleart wool to meet the stringent specifications of the museums, including extremely broad colour needs. The line now contains the widest colour range of Persian yarn in the world and was used to stitch many of the projects in the book.

In the early years of It's Polite to Point®, I began by working with regional museums. Today I work with more than 60 of the most prestigious institutions in the world, including Winterthur Museum, Garden and Library, the Smithsonian Institution, National Trust for Historic Preservation, Museum of Fine Arts, Boston, Royal Ontario Museum, The Art Institute of Chicago and the World Wildlife Fund. Their education and marketing personnel review and approve each of my designs, prior to their release. In addition, they evaluate and select the educational text supplied with every design to explain its history and significance.

After almost twenty delightful years of working with museums, searching through and adapting designs from many of the finest historical collections, this book demonstrates the lessons I have learned about design – that it is part history and part innovation and that all cultures interconnect in many ways. I also share some of the knowledge I have gained about the relationship between history and art. Through the text accompanying the projects, you'll learn telling details about the lives of early peoples. And by continuing the tradition of needlework, you, in turn, will offer glimpses of what your life, generation and personality are like to future generations.

These splendid designs of a gold-coat horseman (top) and red-coat horseman (below left) are derived from a series of tapestries stitched in America in the middle of the eighteenth century. I also stitched the red-coat horseman with multi-stitches for greater variety (below right). You'll find more details in the Fishing Lady chapter (page 28).

WINTERTHUR

I view Winterthur Museum, Garden and Library as I do a luxuriant piece of embroidery. With careful attention to design, colour and proportion, like tiny stitches, the details of Winterthur are meticulously executed and composed in harmonious balance to portray its vision in one exquisite treasure.

Winterthur is a living tapestry where the background fabric is the rolling Delaware countryside of meandering streams, velvety meadows, and majestic trees; the needle and tools are the talented and dedicated staff that draw humankind, art, history, education and nature together; the threads added are the priceless treasures collected and displayed; the embellishments are the nine-storey mansion and historic buildings; and the visionary designer and embroiderer was Henry Francis du Pont.

Winterthur is much more than simply a museum. Set in a grand landscaped estate of more than 900 acres, Winterthur encompasses gardens, a research centre and academic library, conservation laboratories, historic buildings and a community gathering place. It is only with an accumulation of experience that one comes to know fully the many layers, the spirit and energy of Winterthur.

The History

Between 1810 and 1818, the land comprising the original Winterthur estate was acquired by E. I. du Pont, whose family's industrial achievements have an important place in American history. In 1837 James Antoine Bidermann and his wife, Evelina Gabrielle, daughter of E. I. du Pont de Nemours, acquired the estate, northwest of Wilmington, Delaware. They named the property after the town of Winterthur (pronounced Winter-tour), Switzerland, the ancestral home of the Bidermann family. After building their house in the popular Greek-revival style, they devoted much time to the development of the landscape.

The estate eventually passed to Bidermann's nephew, Henry Algernon du Pont and then to his son, Henry Francis du Pont, who inherited the estate on his father's death in 1926. He continued and greatly expanded the work of his predecessor in the garden and farm. He also increased the tempo of his own antique collecting, which had begun in earnest around 1923. He decided to collect American antiques, believing that they had not been given the recognition that they deserved. He assembled examples of architecture, furniture, and widely divergent early-American objects and materials of all kinds.

Henry F. du Pont was passionate in his collecting and chose to display his treasures creatively and actually live with them. He and his family lived in a museum-in-progress. His children grew up surrounded by beautiful, breakable objects amid the sounds and sights of construction as du Pont collected for and installed 175 period room settings and display areas. He opened the estate as a public museum in 1951, to share with others the culmination of almost thirty years of ambitious and passionate collecting. Today Winterthur houses the

Above: the stately mansion of Winterthur viewed through the garden.
Right: Readbourne Parlour, just as Henry Francis du Pont set it out.
Courtesy of Winterthur Museum.

world's premiere collection of decorative objects made or used from 1640 to 1860 in the USA.

While many museums exist merely as repositories for collections that reside in frozen galleries, Winterthur Museum possesses a special magic that is the result of an emphasis on the interpretation of craft and culture. Henry F. du Pont injected vitality into Winterthur by collecting only the finest, rarest or key pieces and then bringing the visitor into close contact with them. He preferred authentic and documented pieces, seeking out and recording the stories associated with the objects. This preservation and promotion of learning reflected his vision of more than just collecting.

Just as important as the acquisition of the right objects was their arrangement in appropriate settings so that they demonstrate their decorative or utilitarian value. He enlisted the foremost scholarly and professional assistance for the arrangement of the rooms, selecting accessories and locating precedents and prototypes for his architectural arrangements. His concern with authenticity and historical accuracy is a testament to the seriousness of his intention and to his maturity in the field of collecting.

Each of the 175 rooms underwent countless changes and experiments as du Pont sought just the right blend of furniture, ceramics, textiles, metals, and paintings. Whether the room was baroque, rococo, oriental or neoclassical, he was equally attentive to the regional and historical accuracy of the rooms he created. Travelling widely to locate pieces, everything in the rooms was then carefully scrutinized and meticulously arranged.

Once he determined that the exact types and positioning of objects were archaeologically correct, their spots were identified with small markers, some hammered into the floor. This ensured that the precise effect would be perpetuated. He kept detailed layout plans and

inventories of rooms, including lists of textiles and rugs in many variations according to seasonal changes and occupancy patterns.

Much as a stitcher creates embroidery, he used the antique architectural elements he installed as a canvas and mixed colour, textures and design to achieve a masterpiece. This would permit guests to experience first-hand, rather than simply view, history. By the time of his death in 1969 du Pont had assembled a collection of more than 59,000 items, considered the best in the world in quality, variety and depth. However, it did not stop then. Believing that the collection would never be finished, Henry F. du Pont created the dynamics for a continuing legacy. He left instructions to trustees of his estate and museum, listing many types of objects that had eluded him and that he hoped would eventually be acquired.

The museum professionals who have carried on his vision have added dramatically to Winterthur's material and historical riches. The vast collections of Winterthur are more than just a litany of the best Anglo-, German-, and Dutch-American artistry and craftsmanship. They are a tool that du Pont felt could provide telling insights into the lives of early Americans. The objects he collected were not only those that Americans made, but heirlooms which they brought with them from many cultures. For me, and the guests who experience Winterthur, this remarkable collection offers an unequalled source for a better understanding of American history and how it was shaped by a melting pot of cultures that established themselves as one nation.

Perpetuating the Legacy

One of the most important features for me, as an adaptation specialist, is the people who are at Winterthur today. Perpetuating the unique legacy of Henry Francis du Pont is a successful and thriving community of people who maintain a constant state of activity and change at Winterthur with the same discipline and passion for perfection as Henry F. du Pont.

This group continually adds to the collections, knowing that new objects enhance Winterthur's ability to delight, inspire and educate guests. The analysis, design, digging, weeding, pruning, planting and evaluating of the gardens also contributes to the feeling of being in a living, ever-changing, fresh environment.

Like the gardens, the buildings at Winterthur need care as part of a comprehensive plan to maintain structural stability, historic integrity and beauty. Important restoration and building projects are ongoing to help ensure that the long-term survival of Winterthur's many treasures is secure for future generations.

Throughout the year the grounds are opened for events such as steeplechase races, elaborate picnics, seasonal festivals, craft fairs, handicraft classes and concerts. The Winterthur staff continually develop new and innovative programming, always looking at how to enhance the ways visitors can learn from the experience.

My Connection with Winterthur

As an adaptation specialist, I have found Winterthur to be a captivating and significant experience. It is a dynamic, changing environment in which one may examine unparalleled riches and be filled with inspiration. By understanding its true nature, I can more fully understand the artistry, tastes and personalities of those who made or used the original objects from which I compose my designs. Hence, I like to think that my translations reflect what life was like in early America and how lives were affected by the unlikely combination of the vast cultural influences that created America.

Staff at Winterthur contributed to the creations in this book, ensuring that each design reflects Winterthur's mission and instructs the public. Although the designs may be adaptations or interpretations of past designs, modified in colour, proportion or materials, they preserve the spirit of the originals.

As a collector, gardener, and individual, Henry Francis du Pont always looked to the future and undreamed-of opportunities. I hope that I convey in this book a small part of his spirit and the magic of Winterthur. I encourage you to infuse his creative energy into your needlework and to discover new possibilities for yourself. If you are able to visit Winterthur, I encourage you to do so.

BASIC TECHNIQUES

Many experienced stitchers will overlook this section, thinking it is just elementary education. However, it contains many tips for easier and better stitching. If you read little else in this book, I suggest you at least peruse this section.

Canvas and Fabric

Quality needlepoint canvas is made of woven cotton treated with size (sizing) for added stiffness, strength and smoothness. Poor-quality canvases can be too harsh on your fibres and too limp for even tension and proper finishing. Mono and interlock canvases are the most popular types and are used in most needlepoint projects in this book.

Mono canvas has single vertical and horizontal threads. The threads can slide, making it the best choice for seat covers, church kneelers and other projects that must give regularly to uneven pressure. Good-quality mono canvas is smooth and easy on yarns, and the canvas holes are clearly visible. However, it frays more easily and doesn't keep its shape as well as interlock.

My favourite canvas is interlock which has a single horizontal thread and double vertical threads. These double threads twist around each horizontal thread, locking them in place. This makes the canvas more resistant to distortion while stitching and it holds its shape longer after blocking.

Quality evenweave fabrics are similar to canvas, but the threads are closer together, thinner and softer. Aida is a cross-stitch fabric I would recommend for beginners. The holes are plainly defined and therefore easy to count. When you become more experienced you can try finer fabrics like linen.

Fabric Count and Mesh Sizes

The projects in this book are worked on a variety of evenweave fabrics and needlepoint canvases in a range of count or mesh sizes. The count or mesh size refers to the number of holes to every 2.5cm (1in) of fabric. Evenweave fabrics have the same number of horizontal and vertical holes in every 2.5cm (1in) square, making it easy to count threads and make your stitches uniform. If you count 14 holes along 2.5cm (1in) of your fabric, it is 14 count; if canvas, it is called 14 mesh. The higher the number of holes per 2.5cm (1in), the closer the threads, and the smaller the stitches will be. Fabrics range from three holes per 2.5cm (1in), a canvas suitable for large designs such as rugs, all the way to 50-count silk gauze for miniature projects.

Fibres

Threads are available in a wide variety of weights, materials and colours. Fragile threads should not be used for a piece exposed to heavy wear, such as a chair seat. A framed piece, however, allows greater latitude for creative fibre use. Different fibres can be combined for striking effects, but require patience because control is more difficult when using two fibres of different elasticities.

Persian yarn is my favourite because it can be used with a large range of fabric gauges and it comes in an extensive colour range – almost 500 different shades. You can strip the three, easily-separable plies and use from one-ply for petit point or counted cross stitch, to a combination of several plies to cover large canvas meshes. You can even combine plies from more than one colour for wonderful effects.

Tapestry yarn is also a popular choice. Made of four tightly twisted plies, it has a smooth finish. The plies are not separable, which limits its versatility in adapting to various mesh sizes. The thickness of tapestry yarn varies from brand to brand, so you must work a sample to determine the proper size mesh to use. Tapestry yarn is generally worked on #10, #12, #13 or #14 mesh only. It is softer and therefore less durable than Persian yarn, so it has a tendency to fluff up and wear thin if you use too long a strand.

Crewel yarn is thin, fine, non-separable two-ply single-strand yarn. It is adaptable for finer meshes or can be twisted with tapestry or Persian yarn.

Knitting yarn should be used in short lengths, only as accents, because it is not as durable as other yarn types. Watch stitch tension since these fibres are elastic and tangle easily.

Rug yarn is a bulky, heavier weight, non-separable yarn for use with large mesh canvases. It comes in limited colours.

Embroidery cotton (floss) is used for counted cross stitch and with smaller mesh canvas. It is adaptable for a large range of fabric gauges and it comes in many colours. Not as durable as wool, it isn't recommended for projects subject to hard wear. Strip apart the six separable plies before stitching for even coverage.

Pearl cotton is a lustrous, softly twisted cord. The plies are not separable, so if it doesn't fit your chosen mesh size, try using two sizes together. It comes in four sizes – the larger the size number, the finer the cord.

Matt cotton is a soft, supple, heavy embroidery twist without a lot of sheen.

Silk has greater strength than cotton and is smoother so it is easy to pull through fabrics. It also maintains its lustre, strength and colour better than cotton. A project stitched with silk should be dry-cleaned only and should not be wet-blocked. Wetting it will destroy its sheen. It is expensive and not recommended for hard wear.

Rayon produces an effect similar to silk, though often with a higher gloss. It is generally cheaper than silk.

Metallic fibres have been used in embroideries for many centuries. Today's threads often consist of an outer metallic casing wrapped around an inner core. They can be difficult to use as they are fragile, especially when pulled through rough canvas, and you will need to use short threads. Make sure you buy non-tarnishable threads.

Double-sided ribbon can be stitched with a #20 tapestry needle. Cut ribbons on a sharp diagonal to lessen fraying and make them easier to thread. When using various fibres, complete the ribbon areas first.

Novelty fibres are used primarily for accents or for small projects. They can be challenging to work with and difficult to block, but the benefits are often worth the effort. Linen threads, crochet cotton, string, raffia, nylon tubing, even human or animal hair can give interesting textures but do not always wear well. Follow the manufacturers' suggestions for the proper use of all novelty fibres and experiment before using them in a final project.

Needles

Tapestry needles have blunt points so they will not split the canvas threads and an eye large enough to accommodate the yarn. The correct needle size is determined by the mesh size. I suggest #18 needles on #10 and larger meshes, #20 needles on #12 mesh, and #22 needles on #13, #14, and #18 mesh canvas. For cross stitch on evenweave fabrics I use a size #24 or #26 tapestry needle. Use the needle size you are most comfortable with but make sure the eye does not spread the fabric holes too far.

Frames

Many people stitch their stresses into their needleart, working tightly and yanking their projects drastically out of shape. While I applaud using needleart for therapy, you may be disappointed if you can't reshape your needlework. I recommend frames or hoops for anyone who, after their first few pieces, discovers that they will not block easily, nor hold a good blocking. Note, however, that many multi-stitches call for free manipulation of the cloth, making them easier to work without a frame.

Preparation

Before stitching your design, fold masking tape over the edges of your fabric or canvas to prevent fraying or fibres catching. Many people caution against using tape, but with ample margin, you will cut away any sticky fabric. Alternatively, hem the edges or bind them. Write 'top' on the tape with a waterproof marker to ensure your stitches run in the same direction.

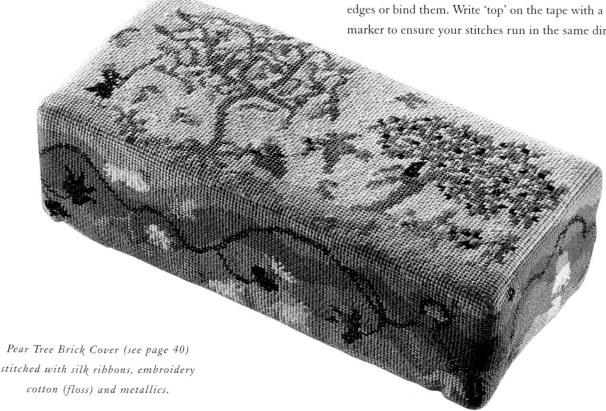

Pear Tree Brick Cover (see page 40) stitched with silk ribbons, embroidery cotton (floss) and metallics.

Using Threads Correctly

Cut your wool strands about 45cm (18in) long – any longer and they are likely to twist, knot and separate or break. If you have any of these problems anyway, use shorter strands. With soft or more delicate speciality fibres use just 20-30cm (8-12in) at a time.

Thread the first length of yarn and pull the needle up through your fabric, leaving a tail about 2.5cm (1in) long on the wrong side. Catch this tail to secure it with the first few stitches. Weave each successive thread length under every other stitch, until it is secured under four or more stitches on the fabric's wrong side, close to where stitching will resume. You can similarly end the threads by weaving them through the back of several nearby stitches, then trimming close to the canvas for a neat finish.

Also weave under stitches on the back when jumping from one area to another with the same colour. When jumping a colour more than 2.5cm (1in) it is best to use a fresh thread length. Never pass your thread behind an unworked area of canvas and do not weave dark thread behind light-coloured areas or you will see an unattractive shadow on the front of your finished piece.

To help prevent the thread twisting and tangling, I give the needle a half turn before each new stitch. You may also need to hold the canvas up to let the thread dangle and untwist itself at intervals. Gradually slide your needle along your thread as you stitch – leaving the needle in the same position throughout will fray one spot.

When my fabric gauge requires an even number of plies, I take half the designated number and thread the needle, pulling the plies until the ends meet (fig. 1). This makes it much easier to control tension, since the needle pulls on all plies equally. The only disadvantage of doubling over the threads is that when you need to remove a stitch, it is harder to back it out. In this case, cut the needle off the end and thread the required number of plies through the needle, leaving a tail dangling in the usual fashion (fig. 2). For an odd number of plies, use the conventional method of threading, leaving a tail dangling.

Stitching Methods

There are two stitching methods: sewing and stab-stitching. In the sewing method, dip the needle down under the fabric and back up, pulling the thread through in one motion. To stab-stitch, pull the needle and entire thread down through the fabric first, then pull them up in a second motion.

These methods are interchangeable. However, frames limit you to the stab-stitch method which also tends to distort the canvas less. Because I have had a great deal of practise, I use the sewing method almost exclusively, without a frame. Eventually, with discipline and patience, you too may use this method. Note, however, that the use of a frame and the stab-stitch method are recommended with most speciality fibres because they are delicate.

Stitching a Project

The materials list for each project contains at least 120% of the yarn used to stitch the original. This accommodates both basketweave and continental stitching styles as well as most multi-stitching techniques. Most projects are stitched with Persian yarn. Use a full three-ply strand for #10 mesh, separate one ply for stitching #18 mesh and use two plies for #12, #13 and #14 mesh. Do not discard any plies you are not using – save them to utilize later.

All the charts may be used for needlepoint, cross stitch or multi-stitching. Unless you are working multi-stitches or bargello, each chart square represents one tent or one complete cross stitch.

You can begin anywhere on the chart, except for bargello which is worked from the centre outwards. Other than for bargello, always work from the finest details to the next largest areas, whether working one colour throughout or one area of the design at a time. With needlepoint, always work lighter backgrounds last so they do not become soiled from handling or pick up hairs from darker yarns.

On occasion, it may be helpful to turn your piece 180 degrees, but be sure to turn the chart as well. Never turn your work by only 90 degrees or your stitches will not run in the same direction.

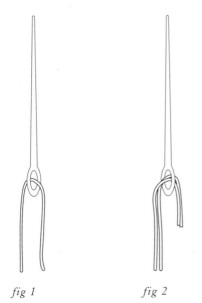

fig 1   *fig 2*

Before beginning a project, consider how the item will be mounted or finished (see Finishing Techniques, page 120). You may need to work additional rows for hems and seam allowances.

Stitches

Most of the projects are worked in tent stitch (needlepoint), a highly durable stitch which is small enough to portray detail, depth, light and shading accurately. However, if you prefer, you can use other stitches instead – cross stitch, for example, or multi-stitches.

There are three methods of working tent stitch: horizontally, vertically and diagonally. The horizontal and vertical tent stitches are known as continental stitch. The diagonal tent stitch is called basketweave stitch because of its appearance on the wrong side. Diagonal tent stitch is the easiest to block and distorts the canvas least. On the right side all stitches must slope in the same direction.

I tend to use the most yarn possible for all stitches, travelling to the furthest end of the next stitch. This allows me to pad the back as thoroughly as the front, which should add to the longevity of the piece. However, if you prefer you can

A variety of fibres were used to make this Lattice and Flowers design purse and bag (see page 58).

make the shortest connections on the back. The illustrations show the needle positions for my longer stitching method. For the thread-saving version, work the stitches 1 to 2, 2 to 4, 4 to 3, 3 to 5, and so on.

Left-handers can use the stab-stitch method, following the stitch diagrams as they appear or use the sewing method, working with both the canvas and stitching diagrams upside down and following the same number order.

Working Multi-stitches

To work a variety of stitches on canvas, first draw an outline of the design on the canvas with a light-coloured indelible marker. To work on evenweave fabrics, tack (baste) this outline on the fabric. Follow the graph provided with the project as a guide to thread colours.

Your multi-stitches need not meet the outline exactly. You can decide whether to stay within it or to go slightly beyond it, depending on the size of a stitch or the number of threads it covers. You can also work partial stitches where necessary.

Stitching Techniques

Follow these instructions to work a variety of stitches. In the illustrations, odd numbers indicate the needle coming to the front from the back and even numbers indicate the needle going to the back from the front.

Horizontal tent stitch (continental)

Work from right to left. Rotate the canvas top to bottom after the last stitch of each row to continue stitching the next row from right to left. Don't forget to rotate your chart too.

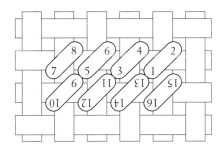

Vertical tent stitch (continental)

Work towards yourself. Rotate the canvas top to bottom after the last stitch in each row, so you can continue stitching towards yourself on the next row. Rotate your chart too.

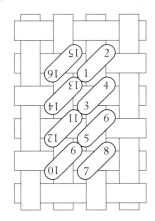

Diagonal tent stitch (basketweave)

Start in the upper right-hand corner and work across the canvas in ascending and descending diagonal rows. You will see a triangular pattern develop. You need not turn the canvas between rows.

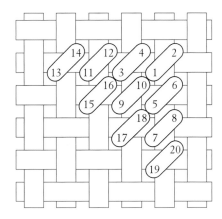

Cross stitch

Always make the same part of the two-part stitches in the same order and direction throughout your piece. Either make all the bottom stitches first and then come back and make the second part of the cross stitch (top), or make each stitch complete each time, ensuring you always begin with the same part of the stitch (below).

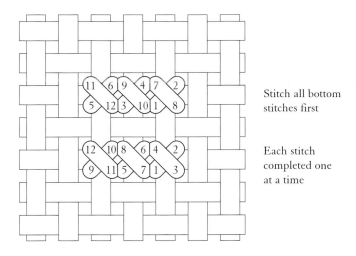

Stitch all bottom stitches first

Each stitch completed one at a time

Back stitch

Take a small backward stitch through the fabric, then bring the needle up a little way in front of the first stitch and repeat so the stitches touch end to end.

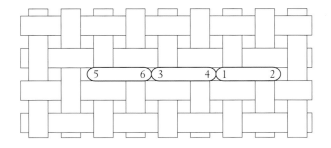

Brick stitch

Work in descending or ascending rows as shown. (See also Beautiful Bargello, page 44).

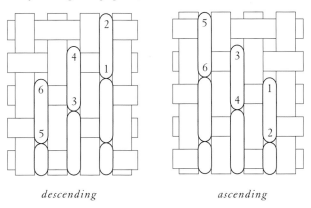

descending   *ascending*

Bullion *(see fig. overleaf)*

Make a long stitch, 1.3-2.5cm (^{1}/2-1in) long, from 1 to 2, leaving a loop on the surface of the fabric; bring the needle partway up at 1 and twist the thread around the needle, until the number of twists equals the distance between 1 and 2.

15

Pull the needle through this coil, flattening it down against
the fabric, insert the needle at 2 and pull firmly.

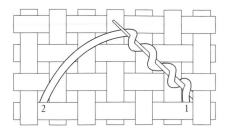

Chain stitch

*Bring the needle out at 1 and reinsert it at the same point,
leaving a loop. Bring the needle out at 2 to catch the loop
and make the first chain. Each stitch is tied down by the
stitch that follows it.*

Couching

*Anchor a main line of thread (1-2) with perpendicular
stitches, about every 6mm ($^1/_4$in). The main line and anchor
stitches can be the same colour or contrasting colours.*

Cretan stitch

*Work this stitch as shown, flipping the loop from side to side
as you work along the length of a leaf, for example, to prevent
the thread twisting the wrong way.*

Cross with a back stitch

*Work this stitch in the order shown, starting with a cross
stitch and then adding a horizontal bar.*

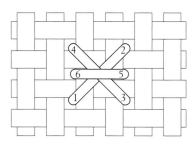

French knot

*Come up at 1 and wrap the yarn once around the needle; go
down at 2, keeping tight tension on the yarn. You may also
wrap the needle twice for a bolder effect.*

Long/straight stitch

Work long stitch as shown. Straight stitch is a variation in which the stitches can be any length, and run vertically, horizontally or randomly.

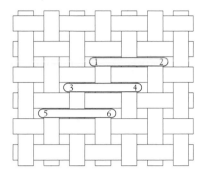

Mosaic stitch

Work this stitch as shown.

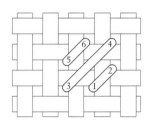

Outline stitch

Work as shown. The thread may be held either to one side of the needle or the other, but once a line is started always hold the thread to the same side. When outlining a curve, hold the thread away from the shape, toward the outside of the curve. This will make the curve smoother.

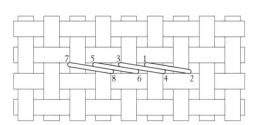

Ray

This stitch radiates from a single point. Each time you bring the needle up it should be at 1.

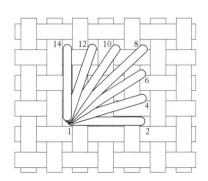

Running stitch

Running stitch is a stitch used to join two pieces of fabric. Run the needle in and out of the fabric. I use this stitch for joining pieces of fabric or needlework instead of back stitch.

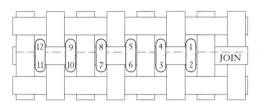

Slanting Gobelin

Work this stitch as shown.

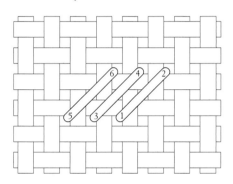

Turkey knot

Work in horizontal rows. Begin with about 2.5cm (1in) hanging on the surface of the fabric. After filling the shape, cut off the loop tops, trimming the whole shape to the desired length.

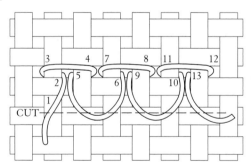

Upright cross

Work this stitch as shown, finishing each stitch completely before starting the next (compare with cross stitch).

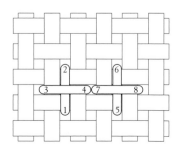

ALTERING THE COLOURWAY

I plan everything about the colour of my projects carefully, taking into account the intended use of the piece. For example, I selected a pale background for my Cornucopia rug because it will rest on a dark floor. For a rug in a highly travelled pathway, a medium to dark colour is more practical.

Our perception of a colour is affected by surrounding colours, so I always start by selecting my background or the largest-area colour. Then I add other colours, one family at a time. Occasionally, at the end of the palette selection, I will alter the background slightly, though usually only one value (lightness or darkness), or I may switch to the same value in a similar family. If you change one or two colours, always gather the entire palette of fibres together again to check the effect.

If you wish to change a colourway, I recommend that you replace the values of one colour family with the same values of another – changing a group of strawberry reds to a group of mauve reds, as demonstrated in the Birds & Butterflies table runner (page 52), for example. Ensure that all the colours are still compatible.

The more colours in a composition, the more difficult it is to achieve colour balance, so try making changes first on the projects with fewer colours, such as the Victorian Paisley bookmark (page 99). Even when purchasing any of the listed fibres, lay out all the colours together because varying dye lots could slightly alter the overall appearance of a palette. Make any adjustments necessary.

Different types of fibres will affect the palette as well, even if they match the original colour indicated. Glossy surfaces reflect more light than dull surfaces, so the same colour appears different when smooth, rough or metallic. For this reason, fibres also look different when worked with different stitches. You may find that speciality threads are most effective when used for creative stitches because the surface area will be larger to interact with light. As usual, always experiment first, testing for effect and appropriate number of plies.

Most fibre colours appear darker when stitched, so work a test piece to check your choice. Because of the concerns about context with colour, determine which colours touch each other the most and place them next to each other on your scrap to check that they go well together.

Inspiration File and Journals

I believe the ability to select and manipulate colour is inherent in all of us. However, until you are more confident, follow the lead of others. Study the designs of wallpaper, fabrics, wrapping papers, floor tiles, and gift cards. These all have fine examples of colour harmonies. Keep a file of ideas for inspiration, as well as a journal of past projects. There is no substitute for knowledge about colour, gained from one's own personal observation.

I gave the tulip and lily designs from the Victorian Country Garden Bouquets (page 80) a whole new look simply by changing the background colour from creamy beige to dark brown. This simple alteration has a dramatic effect.

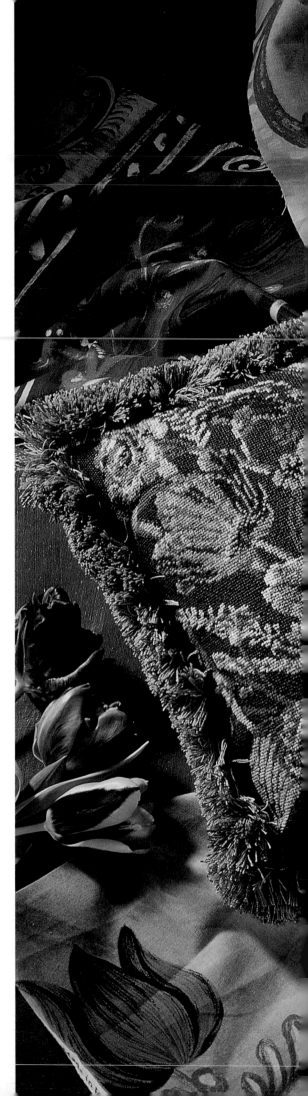

Berlin Bouquets

THE VIBRANCY OF A PREVIOUS ERA COMES ALIVE IN THESE DESIGNS, ADAPTED FROM A SET OF 80-COLOUR BERLIN CHARTS AT WINTERTHUR. ALTHOUGH SIMPLIFIED – WITH JUST 24 STUNNING COLOURS – THE DESIGNS ARE AS SPECTACULAR AND EXCITING AS THE ORIGINALS.

In the Winterthur library I found some of the most exquisite Berlin charts that I have ever viewed in American museums. The twelve-chart collection was a recent acquisition and reflects Winterthur's commitment to carrying on the legacy of Henry F. du Pont in obtaining only the finest pieces. I especially love Berlin charts because I feel that I carry on the Berlin tradition through my charted books and leaflets. I even continue to hand-colour my charts like the original Berlin chartists, although I use coloured pencils and markers rather than watercolours which they used.

The art of Berlin wool work began in 1804 or 1805, when a print seller in Berlin, named Philipson, published a hand-coloured design on graph paper for needlework. There had been designs on similar paper before, but it was rare to find any indication of colour or thread choice. The new Berlin patterns were printed in black ink on point paper, a good-quality graph paper, and then hand-coloured. A brush with a square-cut end and watercolours gave the best results. Minute symbols in the printed patterns marked the shapes of forms, but not the shading, so it was necessary for the colourist to have an artistic eye for both line and colour.

Embroidery worked by copying these coloured charts became known as Berlin wool work. The attraction of the Berlin patterns was not only their beauty, but also that they freed stitchers from the complicated process of developing their own design. Yet there was still room for genius to exert itself in the selection, arrangement and combination of colours as each stitcher personalized the charts with his or her preferences. The type and quality of fibres they selected also influenced the outcome of a project, as you learn in this book.

The other characteristic of Berlin embroidery was the introduction of wools that were softer, thicker and more brilliantly coloured than earlier yarns. Indeed, Berlin work became so popular that manufacturers of materials adapted their products to it. Canvases became coarser and were made using a coloured thread every tenth space on the tan canvas, enabling the needlewoman to count squares more easily and thus transfer the design more quickly.

Though originating in Germany, the English laid the foundation for the

These simplified versions of two Berlin wool work designs capture all the colour and exuberance of the originals. Make the shell design (top left) or anemone (top right) into cushions or extend your work to cover a footstool (bottom).

world-wide success of Berlin wool work through their passionate adoption of this needleart. In 1831 Victorians began a love affair with Berlin wool work, which became so popular that it displaced most other forms of fancy needlework for almost fifty years.

The effects of the Industrial Age contributed to its immediate success. As technology advanced and more people acquired wealth, servants took on daily household chores. Berlin work served to fill the many leisure hours of idle Victorian women. It brought a dash of colour into their otherwise dull and restricted lives and provided relief from the rapidly growing technology by encouraging self-expression. To counteract the smothering effects of mechanization, a taste for nostalgia, romanticism and sentimentality ripened and was reflected in the subjects of the Berlin patterns.

The Victorian enthusiasm for working the Berlin patterns spread far and wide to such places as Russia, Sweden, Denmark, Holland, America, Australia and New Zealand. As the Berlin wool work boom gathered momentum, other countries began either importing Berlin wools and patterns or producing their own. Women's fashion papers in Paris, London, Vienna, Berlin, Philadelphia and elsewhere printed patterns and also gave them away as promotional items. In America, as in Europe, Berlin wool work became the most characteristic feature of nineteenth-century embroidery. American ladies knew what was fashionable abroad and quickly adopted the craft.

Styles and Fashions

Most Berlin wool workers used wools in bright German taste, added beads to the designs, and frequently embellished the finished articles with flamboyant cords and tassels. Though tent stitch and cross-stitch were most frequently used, the patterns lent themselves to a variety of other stitches. Mosaic, Florentine, Gobelin and brick were all popular, attractive and covered canvas quickly. Another favourite stitch, called turkey work, created a plush, raised pile. It was clipped in graduated heights to give a realistic sculptural effect to three-dimensional flowers, animals and birds.

Romantic scenes, colourful animals, ornamental and geometric patterns, and an unending variety of lush naturalistic flower designs emerged. Victorian ladies loved to embroider flowers and many of the pieces of Berlin wool work and charts that have survived show brightly coloured bouquets, wreaths and garlands of flowers. By the time Queen Victoria ascended the throne, gardening had become highly fashionable, flowers were news and the Victorians, with characteristic enthusiasm, wanted flowers on everything, particularly their needlework.

Embroiderers applied the colourful Berlin patterns to every conceivable object, from furniture to costumes and all sorts of trinkets for the home, many recommended by fashionable ladies' magazines. Berlin wool work chair seats, waistcoats, pillows, slippers, purses, fireplace cornices, pole screens, bell pulls, curtain ties, purses, brooches, sentimental verses, rugs and pictures were turned out in immense numbers. Stitchers now filled their homes and churches with colourful handwork as never before.

Different periods in history favoured different background colours for Berlin wool work. Until about 1840, sparse, elegant Regency interiors called for shades of cream, straw or pale blue. Tan, coral and cinnamon were also popular. The furniture was classical, elegant and restrained, and room schemes were more delicate. Later in the nineteenth century, decorating colours became richer and heavier as black, crimson, rust or dark blue became more common, as displayed in the two reproductions created for this chapter.

Gradually, a change came over leisured women world-wide. Their ranks steadily dwindled as they became more educated, and unmarried women needed to earn a living. The need for time-consuming pastimes ended. By 1880 needlework, especially Berlin work, was no longer an essential part of a lady's life. Though our romance with embroidery continues, it has become more of a hobby than a full-time activity.

Making the Projects

I have simplified two spectacular Berlin wool charts for the following projects, worked in 24 fabulous colours. These companion patterns will be much easier to work than the originals, yet will be just as stunning. I have worked two as cushions and stitched an extra pattern to mount on a footstool. (To work either design on a footstool you may need to use a different mesh size to ensure the design fits well.)

Because these patterns are so complex, I would suggest that you stay with the standard tent or cross stitch for the majority of the designs (see page 15). You may want to consider a small alternative stitch for the large areas of the background only, though an occasional French knot (see page 16) would not detract. Multi-fibres are encouraged, though I recommend that they be used in small doses, lest you over-complicate the already busy patterns.

To turn your needlework into a smart cushion and trim it decoratively, refer to the finishing instructions on pages 120-123.

The designs in this chapter were derived from two of a twelve chart collection of floral patterns, hand-painted with opaque water-colour on printed card stock. This is the original for the anemone design.

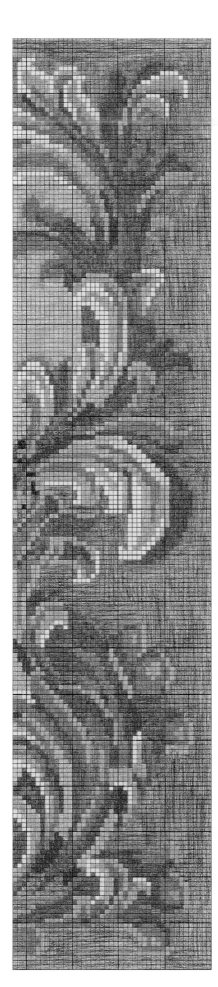

ANEMONE

STITCH COUNT: 199 X 202

FINISHED STITCHED SIZE: APPROXIMATELY 35.5 X 35.5CM (14 X 14IN)

Materials

43.5 x 43.5cm (17 x 17in) #14 mesh canvas (this allows for a 4cm (1¹/₂in) margin
all the way around the design)
No. 22 tapestry needle
It's Polite to Point® Heirloom Quality Needleart Wool in the colours listed below

	COLOUR		1.5M (60IN) LENGTHS REQUIRED		COLOUR		1.5M (60IN) LENGTHS REQUIRED
	WH600	Ivory	5		YL210	Dark rust gold	15
	BR220	Dark chocolate brown	10		YL240	Medium gold	13
	BR030	Medium brown	14		YL720	Bright yellow	6
	OR730	Medium beige peach	3		WH200	Black	24
	OR750	Light peach	5		GN060	Dark blue green	8
	BR630	Medium grey brown	2		GN080	Medium blue green	2
	BR650	Light grey beige	3		GN110	Dark moss green	7
	OR420	Bright red orange	5		GN130	Medium moss green	4
	OR530	Medium orange	2		PP140	Light purple	3
	RD010	Dark maroon	4		BL410	Dark blue	2
	RD040	Medium pink maroon	3		BL440	Medium blue	22
	RD060	Light pink maroon	3		BL460	Light blue	4

Use two of the three plies at a time. For general stitching instructions and conversions
for other mesh sizes, see Basic Techniques, page 11.

Making a Footstool

If you wish to cover a square footstool with this design, measure the stool and adjust the canvas mesh size so that the pattern fits it. Include any padding in your calculations. See Finishing Techniques (page 120) for instructions on lacing the needlework onto the footstool.

SHELL

STITCH COUNT: 199 x 202

FINISHED STITCHED SIZE: APPROXIMATELY 35.5 x 35.5CM (14 x 14IN)

Materials

43.5 x 43.5cm (17 x 17in) #14 mesh canvas (this allows for a 4cm (1¹/₂in)
margin all the way around the design)
No. 22 tapestry needle
It's Polite to Point® Heirloom Quality Needleart Wool in the colours listed below

COLOUR		1.5M (60IN) LENGTHS REQUIRED	COLOUR		1.5M (60IN) LENGTHS REQUIRED
WH600	Ivory	9	YL210	Dark rust gold	4
BR220	Dark chocolate brown	7	YL240	Medium gold	9
BR030	Medium brown	9	YL720	Bright yellow	7
OR730	Medium beige peach	6	WH200	Black	26
OR750	Light peach	5	GN060	Dark blue green	6
BR630	Medium grey brown	2	GN080	Medium blue green	4
BR650	Light grey beige	3	GN110	Dark moss green	8
OR420	Bright red orange	3	GN130	Medium moss green	8
OR530	Medium orange	2	PP120	Dark purple	4
RD010	Dark maroon	7	PP140	Light purple	4
RD040	Medium pink maroon	5	BL440	Medium blue	21
RD060	Light pink maroon	3	BL460	Light blue	4

Use two of the three plies at a time. For general stitching instructions and conversions
for other mesh sizes, see Basic Techniques, page 11.

Making a Footstool

If you wish to cover a square footstool with this design, measure the stool and adjust the canvas mesh size so that the pattern fits it. Include any padding in your calculations. See Finishing Techniques (page 120) for instructions on lacing the needlework onto the footstool.

Fishing Lady Embroideries

THE CHARMING RURAL SCENES SELECTED FOR THESE PROJECTS ARE ADAPTED FROM SEVERAL OF THE MANY FISHING LADY EMBROIDERIES AT WINTERTHUR. THE SCENIC VIEWS WITH DISTORTED PERSPECTIVES ARE TYPICAL OF THE SURVIVING PETIT-POINT TENT-STITCH WORK MADE DURING THE MID-EIGHTEENTH CENTURY WHICH WAS CREATED IN THE BOSTON, MASSACHUSETTS AREA.

As Henry F. du Pont became involved in assembling room settings compatible with the early furniture to be displayed in them, he recognized the significance of the needlearts in the early American home. He studied wills and inventories that listed possessions in order of their importance. Land, money and silverware were the only listings preceding needlework, household textiles and clothing, proving that American needlework sustained high monetary value. Families also treasured needlework items beyond their basic monetary value as textiles because of their important personal associations. Today, the Winterthur needlework collection has grown to more than six-hundred remarkable examples, offering a truly unequalled source for a better understanding of history.

During my many explorations of Winterthur, I became intrigued by a number of different embroidered landscapes with striking similarities. Upon further investigation, I discovered that these captivating scenes were part of a series of important and well-known tent-stitch pictures on linen made in America during the early to mid-eighteenth century. The Fishing Lady was the name given to surviving pieces of the series, of which close to sixty-five pieces have been traced.

The embroideries, originating in the New England area, all feature ladies and gentlemen with a variety of dogs – often up to some mischief – sheep, birds, deer and imaginative flora set against pastoral landscapes, always with a charmingly distorted perspective. The series was named because of the prevalence of a fishing lady motif in many of the embroideries, possibly explained by the popularity of fishing as an eighteenth-century American courting pastime. In addition to scenes of courtship, some of the figures are shown working in the fields, gathered for a picnic, or in miniature hunting scenes.

The Fishing Lady series follows the naturalistic style popular in England from the early 1600s and reflects the inherent love of garden and country which the Colonial needlewoman brought with her from the mother country.

The Colonial lady's love of gardening is revealed in this set of projects based on the museum's Fishing Lady embroideries. The lady is seen fishing (top right) and with a flower garland (below). The alluring fishing lady design has also been mounted onto an attractive tray (top left). Two riders on horseback (shown on page 6) complete the set.

The main elements of the designs in this chapter are clearly visible in this original tapestry (c.1740-60).

An indifference to scale and perspective was a special characteristic of both the British and American embroidered pictures of this period which is often regarded today as quaint. This was the result of adapting patterns from two or more sources, with differing sizes and proportions of motifs, that were all used in one design.

The Fishing Lady embroideries are typically simpler than their British counterparts. Often drawn from the same pattern books, illustrations and engravings as British patterns, the New England landscapes preserve the English flavour, but are peppered with indigenous details. For example, in American versions the houses are accurate depictions of New England architecture, rather than the castles frequently used in English counterparts. Though many figures in both British and American scenes can be traced back to the same original source, the source material for the fishing lady herself still defies identification.

School-day Origins

The repetition of subject matter and details in American Fishing Lady embroideries suggests a common source of design. Mrs Susannah Condy, who ran a shop and boarding school in Boston, was the most likely creator of the pattern. Eighteenth-century newspaper advertisements indicate that she sold materials for needlework and had patterns from London that were redrawn by her, making them much cheaper than English patterns. She probably used the original pattern for many copies, retaining the main figure and her pose, while changing the surrounding design.

Throughout the eighteenth and nineteenth centuries, numerous schools like Mrs Condy's were established along America's eastern seaboard, especially in the most prominent cities such as Boston. As America grew in size and prosperity, a large middle class was created that focused on the increased education of children. For girls, this meant learning not only the basic skills of literacy and numeracy, but also music, dancing, painting, and needlework of the practical and ornamental kind, typically referred to as plain work and fancy work. No girl was thought of as marriageable without mastery of needlework and it was considered alluring to the opposite sex for a young woman to be sitting with a piece of embroidery in her hands.

Most of the more advanced pictorial embroideries were done by girls aged twelve to sixteen at school, where the teacher, such as Susannah Condy, often provided a distinctive pattern that is today easily traced. The Fishing Lady embroideries were probably produced as school graduation pieces, since the stitchers were identified as being in their late teens or early twenties, though one original reveals the artist to be only thirteen. Each piece, usually framed or placed on a chair seat and given a place of pride in the front parlour or sitting room, was, for all suitors to see, a certificate of a young lady's ability.

No better subject existed for these coming-of-age needleworks than those of courtship as depicted in the Fishing Lady embroideries. Perhaps the fishing lady is symbolic of fishing for suitors in the most idyllic environment for the hopeful maidens and their eager suitors. Or maybe, because young women did these embroideries for display, the fishing lady symbolized that the young lady would be a good catch.

Ambitious efforts that often required one year or more to complete, the embroideries ranged in size from 25 x 30cm (10 x 12in) to 1.5m (5ft) panoramas. Most were finely shaded and skilfully worked in tent stitch, with occasional French knots and satin stitches in fine crewel wools, silks and metal threads. The gentlemen often have silver lace buttons and many have shiny black beads for eyes. Some sheep have fleecy French knotted coats.

Though the proportions are rather distorted, the effect of these fine embroideries is quite delightful and at the same time reflects the lives of the young women of Colonial America. The pieces present not just high standards of craftsmanship and design, but also convey something of the taste and personality of those who made them and offer a glimpse of the distinctly American flora, fauna, pastimes and landscapes of the period.

Working with Multi-stitches

I stitched the Red-coat Horseman pattern a second time using a variety of creative embroidery stitches (page 6). This did not require any more wool than the standard tent-stitch version. Refer to Basic Techniques, page 11, for how to work with multi-stitches. Here are details of the stitches I used and the number of plies:

Brick – vertically on tree trunks; 2-ply.

Bullion – butterfly body and details on tree trunks and branches; 1-ply on left-hand tree and butterfly body; 2-ply on right-hand tree.

Chain – lower left-hand flower leaves, clump of foliage just above dog; 1-ply.

Cretan – pear tree leaves; 2-ply.

French knot – dog's eye, birds' eyes, horse's eye, horseman's hair, and all flower centres; 2-ply.

Long – horizontally 3.1 step on house roof; 2-ply.

Mosaic – butterfly wings; 2-ply.

Outline – details on legs of horse, stag and dog; 1-ply.

Ray – leaves of the right-hand tree and gold areas of left side foliage clump; 1-ply.

Slanting Gobelin – body of horse, stag and dog; 2-ply.

Straight – birds, pears, uppermost dark-blue ground line, house windows, horseman's trousers, stag's antlers, dog's ear and lower left-hand flowers; 2-ply.

Turkey knot – horse's mane and tail; 2-ply.

Upright cross – chimneys and horseman's coat; 1-ply.

Several of the leaves on the left-hand pear tree appear to be variegated, an effect called tweeding. This is achieved by using plies from more than one colour. You can combine plies from different values in the same family for shaded tweeding. You can also combine plies from many different colours for more dramatic effects. I recently stitched an angel Christmas ornament and used plies from gold, yellow and pink cotton (floss) together for the wings to give a luminous effect.

FISHING LADY

STITCH COUNT: 142 X 144

FINISHED STITCHED SIZE: APPROXIMATELY 25.5 X 25.5CM (10 X 10IN)

Materials

33 x 33cm (13 x 13in) #14 mesh canvas (this allows for a 4cm (1¹/2in)
margin all the way around the design)
No. 22 tapestry needle
It's Polite to Point® Heirloom Quality Needleart Wool in the colours listed below

COLOUR			1.5M (60IN) LENGTHS REQUIRED
	BL000	Dark blue	9
	BL040	Light blue	2
	BL210	Dark teal	11
	BL220	Medium teal	11
	GN050	Light green	9
	YL340	Gold	6
	YL040	Light yellow	3
	WH620	Cream	16
	RD310	Dark rose	5
	RD340	Light rose	4
	BR320	Dark brown	4
	BR350	Light brown	7

Use two of the three plies at a time. For general stitching instructions and conversions for other mesh sizes, see Basic Techniques, page 11. Note that the two rose shades and the darker brown are not the same as the ones in the two horseman designs – keep this in mind if you are buying wool for all four designs at the same time.

Making the Tray

Buy your tray before you start the embroidery because you may need to add extra rows to the edges of the design. I added three extra rows of stitching along the bottom to fill the tray opening. You may add the rows to the top or bottom, following the general design. To mount the embroidery, lace the needlework to the base mounting board supplied with the tray (see page 121 for details on lacing).

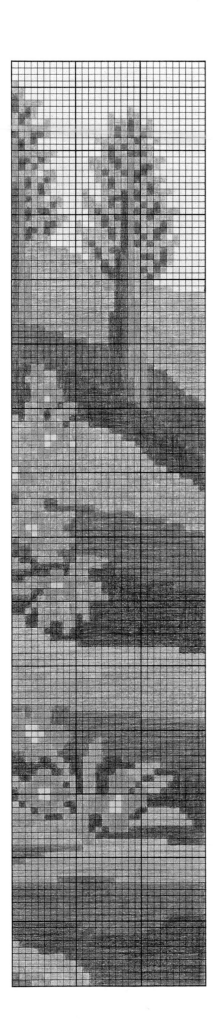

LADY WITH GARLAND

STITCH COUNT: 142 X 144

FINISHED STITCHED SIZE: APPROXIMATELY 25.5 X 25.5CM (10 X 10IN)

Materials

33 x 33cm (13 x 13in) #14 mesh canvas (this allows for a 4cm (1¹/₂in)
margin all the way around the design)
No. 22 tapestry needle
It's Polite to Point® Heirloom Quality Needleart Wool in the colours listed below

	COLOUR		1.5M (60IN) LENGTHS REQUIRED
	BL000	Dark blue	11
	BL040	Light blue	3
	BL210	Dark teal	11
	BL220	Medium teal	13
	GN050	Light green	11
	YL340	Gold	6
	YL040	Light yellow	3
	WH620	Cream	12
	RD310	Dark rose	2
	RD340	Light rose	2
	BR320	Dark brown	2
	BR350	Light brown	4

Use two of the three plies at a time. For general stitching instructions and
conversions for other mesh sizes, see Basic Techniques, page 11. Note that
the two rose shades and the darker brown are not the same as the ones in the
two horseman designs – keep this in mind if you are buying wool for all
four designs at the same time.

GOLD-COAT HORSEMAN

STITCH COUNT: 204 X 197

FINISHED STITCHED SIZE: APPROXIMATELY 35.5 X 35.5CM (14 X 14IN)

Materials

43.5 x 43.5cm (17 x 17in) #14 mesh canvas (this allows for a 4cm (1¹/₂in)
margin all the way around the design)
No. 22 tapestry needle
It's Polite to Point® Heirloom Quality Needleart Wool in the colours listed below

		COLOUR		1.5M (60IN) LENGTHS REQUIRED
	BL000	Dark blue		10
	BL040	Medium blue		6
	BL210	Dark teal		28
	BL220	Medium teal		31
	GN050	Light green		25
	YL340	Gold		7
	YL040	Light yellow		4
	WH620	Cream		34
	RD300	Dark rose		2
	RD320	Medium rose		2
	BR310	Dark brown		9
	BR350	Light brown		12

Use two of the three plies at a time. For general stitching instructions and
conversions for other mesh sizes, see Basic Techniques, page 11. Note that the
two rose shades and the darker brown are not the same as the ones in the two
fishing lady designs – keep this in mind if you are buying wool for all four
designs at the same time.

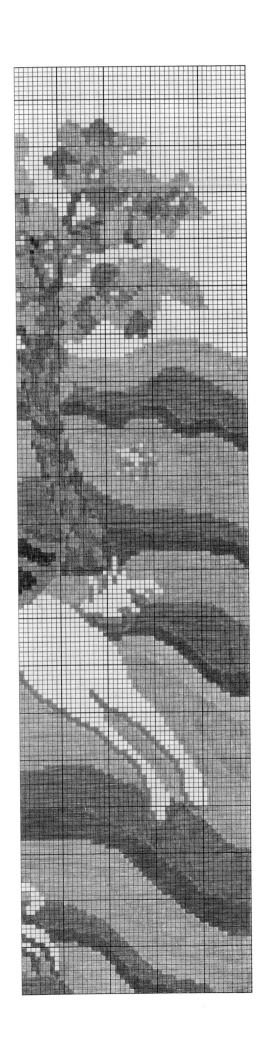

Red-Coat Horseman

Stitch count: 202 x 197

Finished stitched size: Approximately 35.5 x 35.5cm (14 x 14in)

Materials

43.5 x 43.5cm (17 x 17in) #14 mesh canvas (this allows for a 4cm (1¹/2in)
margin all the way around the design)
No. 22 tapestry needle
It's Polite to Point® Heirloom Quality Needleart Wool in the colours listed below

	Colour		1.5m (60in) lengths required
	BL000	Dark blue	13
	BL040	Medium blue	2
	BL210	Dark teal	30
	BL220	Medium teal	31
	GN050	Light green	22
	YL340	Gold	7
	YL040	Light yellow	4
	WH620	Cream	40
	RD300	Dark rose	2
	RD320	Medium rose	3
	BR310	Dark brown	7
	BR350	Light brown	10

Use two of the three plies at a time. For general stitching instructions and
conversions for other mesh sizes, see Basic Techniques, page 11. Note that the
two rose shades and the darker brown are not the same as the ones in the two
fishing lady designs – keep this in mind if you are buying wool for all four
designs at the same time.

Pear Tree Brick Cover

I adapted this pattern from a crewel petticoat border which was splendidly designed and finely executed, revealing the mastery of the craft that the amateur stitcher who worked it obtained. Both the highly artistic use of colour and the humorous quality of the picture provide a sense of the unexpected, revealing the stitcher's vitality. The comical distortions of perspective, distinctive personalities of the animals and other decorative elements create an embroidery that delights the viewer.

A second look at the original piece reveals an almost imperceptible vertical seam that divides the panel into two different styles. The thickness and curve of the meandering vine, the way in which the tree trunks and roots are shaped and embroidered, the number of animals and the varying levels of sophistication in draughtsmanship are different on opposing sides of the seam. Was it stitched in two periods by the same person or was it done by two embroiderers? Perhaps a mother and daughter team or two friends were bound closer by working together.

The panel is typical of eighteenth-century American crewelwork. Particularly in the New England Colonies, women of wealth and leisure and their school-age daughters embroidered brightly coloured patterns on furnishings and clothing using a type of yarn called crewel. Crewelwork, like most embroidery traditions in America, owes a great debt to its English heritage. In general, however, American designs were smaller and less complicated than their English counterparts. The American style was more delicate, and frequently more of the background fabric was visible. The Colonial embroiderer also used fewer, simpler stitches than English needlewomen – many large American pieces displayed only three to five different stitches.

Swift, airy stitches, including feather, herringbone, couching, seed, outline and French knot, were common. Some authorities attribute the popularity of these stitches to the fact that they did not require as much yarn as satin stitch. This was an important consideration during a time when imported crewels were rather expensive. Or perhaps it was because embroiderers more easily mastered these stitches.

At first the only dye available was indigo, so early American crewel workers stitched in blue on bleached white linen. Then they made dyes from woods. The Indian women most likely taught the newcomers about the walnut-husk browns, the pokeberry browns and purples and the yellow saffron that they mixed to get shades of green. Colonial needlewomen dyed their threads with these, and later added cochineal, a dried tropical insect, to make glowing reds. These women became exceptionally skilled in the use of colour, as evidenced in the petticoat embroidery.

Colonial women also gave the old European patterns a new twist. The exotic Chinese, Persian, and East Indian motifs popular in England were often transformed in American interpretations. As she stitched her petticoats, the American embroiderer replaced the tree of life, oriental birds and flowers, peacocks, parrots, lotus, urns and pagodas. She preferred stitching sheep, chickens, corn blades and tassels, wild grapes and pine trees and all the wonders of American flora and fauna.

The long areas on crewel-embroidered curtains, valances and petticoats gave Colonial women the opportunity to create attractive borders. They usually covered them with a vignette, typically portraying figures and animals in a woodland or flowered meadow. Although the designs are balanced, they seldom have repeat motifs.

With the beginning of direct American trade with China following the Revolutionary War, silk fabrics from the Orient became more available and less expensive. The lustre of these fabrics speeded the desire in America to replace the less exotic crewel embroidery. The final blow to crewelwork came during the nineteenth century. The advent of roller printing and cheap woven fabrics during the Industrial Revolution ended the need for decoration by embroidery. Lightly styled furniture with delicate inlays, veneers and glistening fabrics became popular and in this new context, crewelwork seemed old-fashioned.

MAKING THE BRICK COVER

When stitching the two short sides of the design, do not turn the canvas and the chart 90 degrees. Stitch the entire flat canvas with all the stitches running in the same direction, using one ply of the three-ply wool. When the corners are joined, the stitches will run in opposite directions, but on #18 mesh it is not readily apparent. The piece is easier to block and retains its shape better if all the stitches run in the same direction. This advantage outweighs the feature of having the stitches running around the entire finished brick in the same direction.

I restitched the brick cover with silk ribbons, embroidery cotton (floss) and metallics. Because these threads were all used in the form in which they came, not separated into plies, it required three times as much as Persian wool. Refer to Lattice & Flowers, page 58, and Basic Techniques, page 11, for more information on working with multi-fibres. Remember, it is not wise to scrimp on speciality fibres, or they may disintegrate before your very eyes. To finish the brick cover refer to Finishing Techniques, page 120.

This delightful brick cover design is adapted from an American crewelwork panel. Use the covered brick as a door stop, paperweight or bookend.

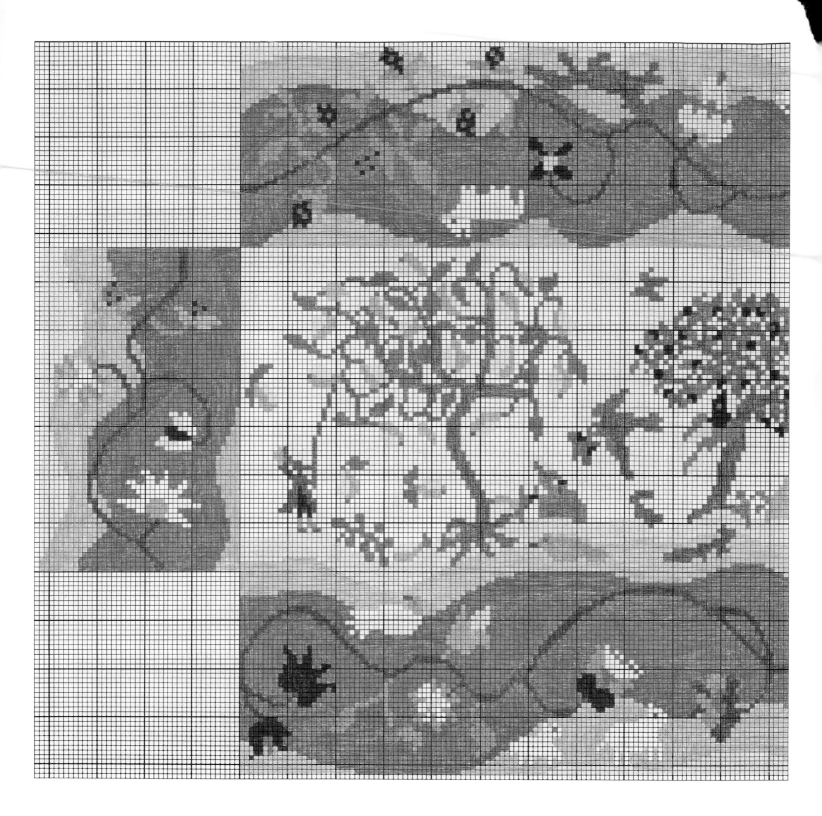

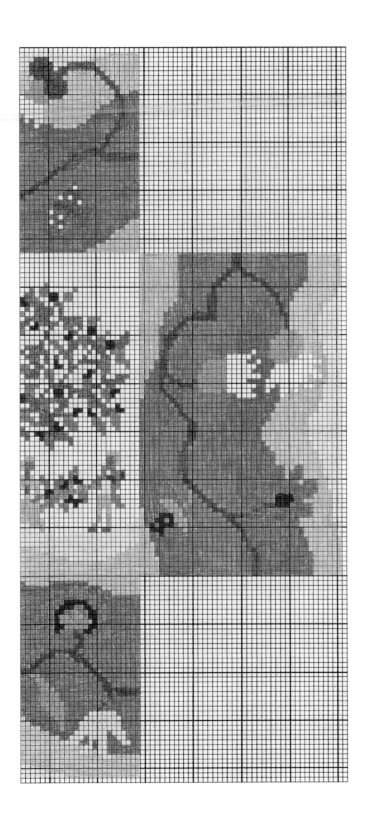

PEAR TREE

STITCH COUNT: 223 X 151

FINISHED STITCHED SIZE: APPROXIMATELY 31.5 X 21.3CM

(12³/8 X 8³/8IN) TO FIT A SMALL BRICK

Materials

38 x 28cm (15 x 11in) #18 mesh canvas (this allows for a
margin just under 4cm (1¹/2in) all the way around the design)
No. 22 tapestry needle
Mediumweight interlining
19.5 x 9cm (7⁵/8 x 3⁵/8in) rectangle of heavyweight felt
Brick or piece of wood 19.5 x 9 x 6cm (7⁵/8 x 3⁵/8 x 2³/8in)
It's Polite to Point® Heirloom Quality Needleart Wool
in the colours listed below

COLOUR			1.5M (60IN) LENGTHS REQUIRED
	BL210	Dark teal	9
	GN270	Medium green	12
	GN130	Light green	9
	YL330	Medium gold	2
	YL040	Light yellow	5
	RD310	Medium rose	2
	RD330	Light rose pink	2
	BL000	Dark blue	3
	BL030	Medium blue	2
	BR350	Medium brown	3
	WH620	Cream	11

Use one of the three plies at a time. For general stitching
instructions and conversions for other mesh sizes, see
Basic Techniques, page 11.

Beautiful Bargello

AMERICAN-MADE IRISH STITCH PIECES INSPIRED THESE ELEGANT DESIGNS. BASED
ON REPETITIVE GEOMETRIC ARRANGEMENTS, THE PATTERNS DANCE ON THE CANVAS
LIKE FLAMES FROM A FIRE.

I first learned bargello as a child and it has remained a passion since my
mother introduced it to me during its last revival in the USA in the late
1960s to early 1970s. When I realized how easy it was to develop a dramatic design quickly, just by counting a simple repetitive motif, I was captivated.
Though there are many practical advantages of bargello – minimal counting, no
costly pre-coloured canvas, minimal yarn requirements and fast stitching – it was
the standard method of using graded shades of colour in vibrant patterns that I
found truly mesmerizing. Experimenting with varying sizes of canvas mesh and
as many colour variations of yarn as my imagination could invent, I applied
bargello to all sorts of projects.

It was not until much later, when I began my career as a needlework designer working with museums, that I discovered enthusiasts through the centuries
had been drawn to bargello for much the same reasons that I had. Today, especially with our time constraints, bargello continues to be a rewarding art. I find
endless inspiration for this at Winterthur, where there are more examples of Irish
stitch than in any other museum that I have visited.

The term bargello is the generic American term for a large variety of upright
stitches. These vertical stitches acquired a confusing assortment of names, perhaps sometime during the late sixteenth or seventeenth century, when significant
creative advances were made in this type of canvas work. Initially found primarily in Hungary, Italy and Great Britain, this European craft spread with the
Colonists to North America where they enthusiastically accepted this stitching
style that they dubbed bargello.

Hungarian point, brick, Byzantine, Irish, cushion, flame and Florentine stitch
were all names used over the centuries to describe the many variations of the long
and short stitches and the steps, or juxtapositions, between them. Bargello has
had a fluid history, assimilating techniques and design motifs of artisans from
many different countries. By any name, in any style, ethnic origin or language, it
is a uniquely creative style.

Conflicting stories obscure the true origins of bargello. Most likely, it was
developed by an embroiderer stitching in wool on coarse, loosely woven cloth,
who found that a larger area of fabric could be covered quickly by working

*A brick-stitch piece is quick to work once you have established the outline. The
original colourway (below) was adapted from an eighteenth-century pocket-
book, but the alternative colourway (top) is equally compelling.*

44

vertical stitches over more than one thread. Possibly having economical concerns, she saw the chance to save wool by 'stepping' these vertical stitches up one and down one thread in the same row, in a delightful staggered interlocking pattern resembling brickwork. Worked in rows across the canvas and not requiring much thought to complete, the stitch produced a smooth, hard-wearing surface. Brick stitch, the logical name given to this early creation, was frequently used by early European embroiderers, especially in Medieval German ecclesiastical work.

A slight variation of the brick stitch evolved, now called the Florentine stitch. It is not done in straight rows across the canvas but in vertical stitches and steps that form peaks and valleys. Then, this slight zigzag row was transformed to a more exaggerated zigzag, and the peaks and valleys grew into 'flames'. It is easy to see why this stitching style was next called flame stitch, since the style and colours made it dance and leap from the canvas much like the flames from a fire.

Hungarian point also emerged as an upright stitch, but the number of mesh over which it is worked may vary from row to row, unlike Florentine, which is worked over a consistent number of threads, row after row. With Hungarian point a very complicated pattern can develop.

At the same time that the flame pattern was prevalent in the seventeenth century, a floral style developed in Italy. It was a true product of the Renaissance, flamboyantly designed with scrolling acanthus leaves, sumptuous realistic and stylized flowers and easily recognizable birds, all worked in Hungarian point with some additional stitches, often against a gold silk background.

While Italian embroiderers were content to rely on foliage strongly influenced by the classical Roman style, English embroiderers found inspiration in their own gardens and Dutch flower paintings. The English worked dense peonies, carnations and other flowers, and stylized foliage in long-and-short, tent, split and satin stitch. They stitched elaborate florals in silks and wools on canvas, with a background of Hungarian point.

By the eighteenth century the bargello stitching style had spread to North America, where it was enthusiastically accepted for a number of reasons. One was that since the designs were not realistic, certain colours, such as green for grass or blue for sky, were not a necessity. It was possible to use whatever colours were on hand. Colonists, whose primary focus was survival, had to be very thrifty and practical. Bargello allowed them to use up all available scraps of materials. This stitching style also reduced the amount of materials necessary to complete a project, thereby saving resources.

As life became easier in the New World and the furnishings less basic and more luxurious, Colonial women began creating more ornamental needlework. They widened the range of decorated items from bed and table covers, curtains, upholstery and ecclesiastical work to include purses, pocketbooks, pockets, shoes, toilet and lace boxes, book bindings, hand-screens, needle-cases and pin-cushions.

Enclosed, repetitive flame-like shapes, all large and complex, were the style in America in the early eighteenth century. As the century wore on, American patterns became smaller, more complex and enclosed: diamond-shaped patterns, carnation patterns and other jagged designs. At the same time, the overall size of the pieces diminished to suit the more modest scale of home decor and the popularity of small projects. Embroiderers used Hungarian point less and less, and instead favoured the Irish stitch and brick stitch. By the end of the eighteenth century the patterns were just 2-5cm (1-2in) high, half what they had been at the beginning of the century.

Stitching Bargello

The bargello stitch used for the following designs is also known as vertical brick stitch. Work each stitch vertically over two threads, stepping one thread up or down for the adjacent stitch. The rows interlock, forming the characteristic 2.1-step regular pattern. To cover the canvas completely in bargello, the bottom of each stitch shares a mesh hole with the top of the stitch below it.

The vertical lines of the chart represent the vertical canvas threads, but each square of the chart represents one horizontal thread. Since the stitch covers two threads, every two vertical squares on the chart represent one stitch. If there are four vertical squares with the same colour, do not cover four threads with one stitch, but make two stitches covering two threads each. Where a single square with a dot is coloured on the diagram work a half stitch, covering one thread vertically.

Begin by folding the canvas in half horizontally and vertically. Where the folds intersect is the exact centre of the canvas. Use the centre mark as a reference for counting the pattern. Working from the centre outwards, stitch your outlines over the entire canvas first. Since the outline is the basis for the rest of the design, work it carefully to avoid a miscount. Check that the repeated portions of the pattern are in line with each other, both horizontally and vertically. Once the outline is stitched, the rest of the pattern will quickly fall into place.

Refer to the diagram on page 15 to work brick stitch in a descending row. Then turn the work and chart 180 degrees to continue working descending rows. If you prefer not to turn the canvas, work an ascending row, again referring to the diagram on page 15. This method of ascending and descending, passing the starting position of the previous stitch to begin the next stitch wherever possible, gives additional padding and covers the meshes better, helping to extend wear.

Stitching the Design

Using the centre of the canvas as a reference for counting, stitch the outline design for the middle horizontal row of medallions first. Work the outline from the centre out to the sides, first to the left, then to the right. Next stitch the outline of medallions above and below. Be sure to use half stitches where marked with a dot within a square. Complete the design, following the chart.

The bargello pattern can be expanded for larger pieces, such as chair seats. Simply extend the design by continuing the basic-motif repeat outward from the centre. You may want to use a larger mesh size if working a large piece. If so, make sure you alter the number of plies accordingly.

Durable yet quick to work, bargello is ideal for large items such as this chair seat which graces the Readbourne Parlour in Winterthur.

AMERICAN MEDALLIONS
BARGELLO

STITCH COUNT: 199 x 164
FINISHED STITCHED SIZE:
APPROXIMATELY 36 x 29CM (14¼ x 11½IN)

Materials

44 x 37cm (17¼ x 14½in) #14 mesh canvas (this allows for a 4cm
(1½in) margin all the way around the design)
No. 20 tapestry needle
It's Polite to Point® Heirloom Quality Needleart Wool in the colours
listed below

COLOUR			ALTERNATIVE COLOURWAY		1.5M (60IN) LENGTHS REQUIRED
	BL730	Black navy outline	GN600	Black green outline	33
	BL010	Dark blue	GN610	Dark green	13
	GN030	Green	BL220	Medium teal	16
	BL980	Medium aqua	GN080	Medium aqua green	17
	BL850	Light aqua	GN090	Light aqua green	7
	RD180	Dark brick	OR700	Dark brick	9
	RD500	Red	OR500	Dark orange rust	7
	RD530	Medium rose	OR630	Medium brick rose	7
	RD340	Pink	OR350	Light peach	7
	WH610	Soft white	RD480	Pale pink white	15
	YL420	Medium gold	BR630	Medium taupe	13
	YL450	Light gold	BR650	Light taupe beige	15
	WH030	Light grey	BR860	Medium brick beige	4

Use all three plies at a time. For general stitching instructions and
conversions for other mesh sizes, see Basic Techniques, page 11.

Alternative Colourway

I restitched the bargello pattern in another colourway to create a softer, lighter effect. Simply convert the chart by replacing the wool shades with the alternative colourway ones.

Birds & Butterflies

ALTHOUGH BASED ON AN AMERICAN-MADE QUILT, THESE DESIGNS SEEM QUINTES-
SENTIALLY ENGLISH, WITH THEIR ELEGANT PEAFOWL AND PRETTY, FRESH COLOURS.
THIS ISN'T SURPRISING, HOWEVER, SINCE THE QUILT-MAKER USED ENGLISH
ROLLER-PRINTED CHINTZES OF THE 1830S FOR HER DESIGN.

Quilting is one of the oldest needlework techniques. Early Eastern cultures, including the Egyptians, Chinese and Turks, all used quilted
materials for warmth, mattresses and for cushioning inside their
armour. The Europeans quilted petticoats and undergarments in the early fif-
teenth century, but by the eighteenth century much less importance was placed
on warmth and utility and much more on the quilt as decoration.

Though quilting is found in many parts of the world, it is widely identified
today as an American cultural tradition. Nowhere else in the world was the
development of quilt-making more dramatically reflected in the history of a
country than in America. Initially, it was simply a practical way of padding
coverlets and putting scrap cloth to good use, but eventually quilting patterns
became more decorative, intricate and creative, characterized by the freshness,
ingenuity and freedom of the Colonies. By the Victorian era the American quilt
was considered the most individual and flamboyant.

The two most popular methods of making quilt tops are piecing and
appliqué. Piecing involves joining fabrics, so many quilts made this way have a
geometric format of squares, diamonds, triangles, rectangles, circles or hexagons.
The top may be composed of anything from a dozen to hundreds or even thousands of shapes, arranged in simple to elaborate patterns.

Appliqué involves stitching small pieces of fabric on top of larger ones.
Because the pieces don't have to fit together, appliqués are not usually geometric
in design, but are more like paintings with fabrics. Wonderful pictorial elements,
flowers, bows, swags, birds, figures and animals are all common themes.

American quilt-makers used printed fabrics regularly in their quilts from
about 1820 onwards, as textile printing technology improved and printed fabrics
became more readily available. They cut appliqué motifs from chintz or other
printed fabrics and applied them to a plain ground (base fabric). They were
influenced by, and imitated, imported Indian fabrics. Quilters created centre

*I pieced together the motifs for these designs in much the same way
as the quilt-maker would have joined pieces for her quilt. The peahen (top
left) and peafowl (top right) are both worked in tent stitch, but I have
repeated the peahen pattern in counted cross stitch (below) to show how
adaptable the charts are.*

The sumptuously flowering branches, exotic birds and gorgeous palette of colours on this appliquéd quilt inspired the peahen and peafowl designs.

designs including Tree-of-Life motifs with peacocks, pheasants and flowering branches framed by one or more borders. Made in more affluent sections of society, particularly in the South and East, the popularity of these show quilts peaked between 1820 and 1840.

The joining of the quilt top with the wadding (batting) and backing was often the occasion for a quilting bee. It was a social function for the women of the community to gather to finish quilts and visit neighbours – an important form of social gathering when neighbours were not too close and did not meet very frequently. These motivations for socializing still bring American quilt-makers together today.

Table Runner and Napkins

I took elements from both the peahen and peafowl designs and worked them in cross stitch to make a table runner and napkin set. I chose a 25-count evenweave fabric for the set and adapted the colourway slightly to coordinate better with it. You can copy the colours I used which are given with the peafowl chart or follow the colourway given for the cross-stitch peahen cushion, if you prefer.

You will need 1.2m (1¼yd) of 140cm (55in) wide 25-count Lugana® cloth from Zweigart® in light rose or your chosen colour. Cut a 43 x 110cm (17 x 43in) rectangle of fabric for the runner and four 48cm (19in) squares for the napkins.

Each stitch is worked with two of the six separable strands of thread over a four-thread square of fabric (two vertical and two horizontal threads), making the scale similar to working on a 12-count fabric (see diagram). On the table runner I stitched the main lower-right motif from the peafowl chart on one end, and the main lower-left motif from the peahen chart at the other end. I scattered the butterflies at random, though not more than 190 stitches (380 threads) from the shorter finished edges.

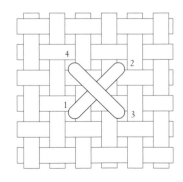

Start by marking the boundaries of the finished edges of the table runner and each napkin with dark tacking (basting) thread 4cm (1½in) from each edge. Follow a fabric thread with your tacking lines to maintain a straight edge.

Begin stitching the table runner with one short edge towards you. I worked the first isolated motif with the stitch furthest to the right beginning on the 30th stitch (on threads 59 and 60) from the right-hand edge of the finished table runner, and on the 26th stitch (on threads 51 and 52) from the bottom. Then I turned the runner 180 degrees and began at the other end, with the second isolated motif, the same number of stitches away from the right-hand side and bottom edges. The uppermost butterflies end on the 190th stitch (on threads 379 and 380) from the finished shorter edges, and no butterflies are placed beyond the side edges of the main design elements.

On each napkin I stitched one butterfly in the lower right-hand corner. Each was placed so that the stitches on the bottom right began on the 9th stitch (threads 17 and 18) from the right-hand finished edge, marked with tacking (basting) thread, and on the 9th stitch (threads 17 and 18) from the bottom finished edge.

Finish the napkins and runner by stitching each one to a matching lining with right sides facing, taking 4cm (1½in) seam allowances and leaving a gap to turn through. You may wish to round off the corners, as I did, to make it easier to add a trim later. Trim the seam allowances, turn right sides out and slip stitch the gap closed. Stitch on a trim, if required. Alternatively, hem the items by turning 6mm (¼in) then 1.2cm (½in) to the wrong side along each raw edge and slip stitching the folds in place.

Designs from the peafowl and peahen charts make delightful cross-stitch motifs for a table runner and napkins. Use the same motifs or copy others from any of the charts in the book.

PEAFOWL

Materials

43.5 x 43.5cm (17 x 17in) #14 mesh canvas (this allows for a
4cm (1¹/₂in) margin all the way around the design)
No. 22 tapestry needle
It's Polite to Point® Heirloom Quality Needleart Wool in the colours listed below

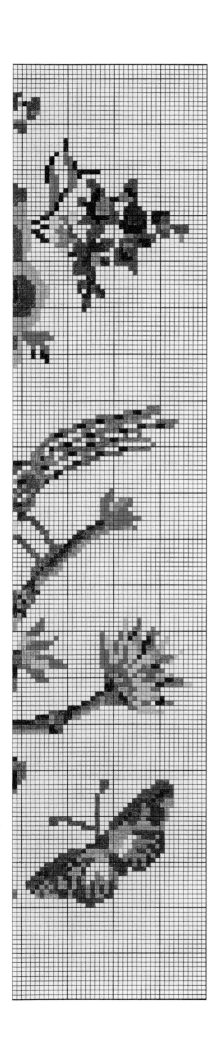

COLOUR			1.5M (60IN) LENGTHS REQUIRED	ALTERNATIVE 8M (8³/4YD) DMC SKEINS
	OR410 (817)	Dark orange red	3	1
	OR430 (350)	Medium orange red	5	1
	OR450 (352)	Light peach	2	1
	BL010 (3750)	Dark blue	3	1
	BL030 (3760)	Medium blue	3	1
	BL050 (519)	Light blue	2	1
	RD300 (221)	Dark rose	3	1
	RD320 (223)	Medium rose	4	1
	RD340 (761)	Light pink	4	1
	BR100 (938)	Dark brown	6	1
	BR120 (975)	Medium brown	9	1
	YL330 (676)	Gold	7	1
	BL200 (924)	Dark teal	8	1
	BL220 (926)	Medium teal	9	1
	WH610 (White)	Soft white	91	1

Use two of the three plies at a time. For general stitching instructions and
conversions for other mesh sizes, see Basic Techniques, page 11.

Table Runner and Napkins

The runner and napkins are worked in cross stitch on 25-count evenweave fabric. Use two
strands of DMC embroidery cotton (floss) with a No. 26 tapestry needle, referring to the
colour numbers above given in brackets and the skein numbers in the last column.

PEAHEN

STITCH COUNT: 198 X 203

FINISHED STITCHED SIZE: APPROXIMATELY 35.5 X 35.5CM (14 X 14IN)

Materials

43.5 x 43.5cm (17 x 17in) #14 mesh canvas (this allows for a
4cm (1¹/₂in) margin all the way around the design)
No. 22 tapestry needle
It's Polite to Point® Heirloom Quality Needleart Wool in the colours listed below

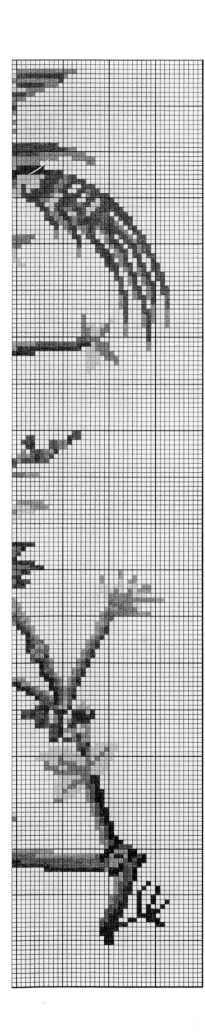

COLOUR			1.5M (60IN) LENGTHS REQUIRED	ALTERNATIVE 8M (8³/₄YD) DMC SKEINS
	OR410 (349)	Dark orange red	4	1
	OR430 (351)	Medium orange red	4	1
	OR450 (754)	Light peach	2	1
	BL010 (336)	Dark blue	5	1
	BL030 (322)	Medium blue	3	1
	BL050 (775)	Light blue	2	1
	RD300 (347)	Dark rose	3	1
	RD320 (760)	Medium rose	5	1
	RD340 (225)	Light pink	2	1
	BR100 (938)	Dark brown	6	1
	BR120 (434)	Medium brown	7	1
	YL330 (729)	Gold	9	2
	BL200 (924)	Dark teal	9	2
	BL220 (926)	Medium teal	8	2
	WH610 (cloth)	Soft white	91	0

Use two of the three plies at a time. For general stitching instructions and
conversions for other mesh sizes, see Basic Techniques, page 11.

Cross-stitch Cushion

Work the cushion in cross stitch on a 43cm (17in) square of 14-count cream or white Aida. Use two strands of DMC stranded embroidery cotton (floss) with a No. 26 tapestry needle, referring to the colour numbers above given in brackets and the skein numbers in the last column.

Lattice & Flowers

THE DESIGNS FOR THIS ELEGANT BAG AND PURSE WERE DERIVED FROM AN ENGLISH ROLLER-PRINTED FABRIC (1820-1825), ALTHOUGH I INTERPRETED THEM IN A DRAMATIC PALETTE WHICH WAS POPULAR SOME TIME LATER.

Popular for curtains and bedcovers in England from around 1815 to 1830, pillar prints are wide-stripe patterns composed of neo-classical columns broken, most frequently, with flowers and baskets. Although these prints never caught on in the rest of Europe, they sold well in America where they were often turned into one-cloth quilts.

The roller-printing technique, pioneered in the early nineteenth century, greatly accelerated cloth printing. The use of faster, more economical printing processes and brilliant mineral dyes, and the choice of pictorial patterns were characteristic of the period. The advent of roller-printing has been called the most important advance in the history of printed cottons. With roller-printing, it became possible to print an entire length of cotton in one mechanical process.

In 1783 Thomas Bell, a Scotsman, patented the first mechanized fabric-printing machine to use engraved metal rollers. Two years later the process was adopted at the English printworks of Livesay, Hargreaves, Hall and Company, near Preston. The six-colour roller-printer did the work of about forty hand-block printers. A similar machine installed in the Oberkampf mill at Jouy-en-Josas in 1797 could print more than 4,572m (5,000yd) of cloth a day, compared to 27.4-91.5m (30-100yd) a day per block-printer. (Production varied according to the number of hours worked, the printer's skill, the number of colours used and the cloth width.)

It was difficult to register (line up) successive colours with several rollers, so monochrome designs imitating copperplate pictorial prints were produced first. Fine patterns or skinny vertical

By stitching the purse and bag in a range of different threads and fibres (back details shown below) you can produce a very glamorous look, ideal for special occasions. Or stitched in high-quality Persian yarn (opposite) they'll last for generations.

repeats were common because of the limited circumference of the rollers – about 30cm (1ft) – but printers eventually adapted equipment to accommodate larger patterns.

By the 1820s most Western mills were using roller printers, and by 1836 American mills alone were turning out about 109,728,000m (120,000,000yd) of printed cloth a year. In the production process, a pantograph transferred designs to a copper cylinder. A diamond point cut through the acid-resistant varnish which coated the cylinder. Then the cylinder was rotated in an acid bath, etching the pattern lines into the copper roller. The cloth ran under the engraved rollers in one long continuous ribbon.

The mechanical developments of roller-printing went hand-in-hand with advances in dye chemistry, dramatically transforming the traditional chintz palette during the first thirty years of the nineteenth century. Until then, most printing was done with vegetable dyes. The first single green was patented in 1809, replacing the traditional but rich double green that had required the overprinting of blue and yellow. By 1830 a whole new range of colours from mineral sources developed. The new dyestuffs were taken up enthusiastically by the industry, resulting in dazzling palettes.

The new textile consumers were the middle and skilled working classes. Even modest households could now afford decorative furnishing fabrics. Printed cotton also allowed all classes of society, from domestic servants upwards, to dress fashionably. The demand for new patterns grew radically. After 1800 fashions in printed cotton changed seasonally for dress patterns and every two or three years for furnishing fabrics. In 1841, in Manchester alone, about 500 people were working as pattern drawers for printed cottons.

The designs themselves were eclectic. Inspiration was sought, as before, in Indian and Chinese textiles and other artefacts, but there was a new interest in classical and Egyptian motifs, particularly in the first decade of the nineteenth century. The period from 1820 to 1850 saw many printed trompe l'oeil designs that imitated woven silks or needlework, stained-glass windows, swagged drapery or passementerie, and architectural details, such as those in the pillar prints. When new ideas were not forthcoming, the pattern drawer would resort to revamping old patterns. Revivals of past styles were a recurrent feature of the period after 1820, encouraged by the taste for revived styles of furniture and interior decoration.

Making the Purse

Follow the chart on page 61 to work the purse design with one strand of the three-ply yarn; block the needlepoint (see page 120). Cut out a piece of lining fabric the same size as the canvas. Pin the lining and needlepoint together with right sides facing. Sew all the way around the edge of the needlepoint, leaving the top front open for turning.

Trim the seam allowances to 6mm (1/4in). Clip off the corners of the seam allowances diagonally, close to the seam. Turn the purse out and slip stitch the opening closed. Iron from the lining side. Fold the purse with the lining on the inside where the lattice area meets the fruits and flowers section. Press the crease only.

Hand-stitch the lattice front to the fruits and flowers back, one side at a time, carefully matching stitch for stitch up the sides. The back section is longer than the front to form the flap. Fold the flap over and press lightly only on the crease. Stitch the three ball halves of the snaps to the purse front, near the bottom of the flap – place one in the centre diamond, skip one diamond in both directions and place another in the next whole diamond in the row containing five complete diamonds and two partials. Sew the socket halves of the snaps to the inside of the front flap to correspond. Your purse is complete.

I restitched the purse in a variety of fibres including silk ribbons and metallics. Because these threads were not separated into plies I required three times as much fibre as Persian yarn.

PURSE

STITCH COUNT: 78 X 132

FINISHED STITCHED SIZE:

APPROXIMATELY 11.5 X 19CM (4$^1/_2$ X 7$^3/_8$IN)

FOR AN 11.5 X 7.5CM (4$^1/_2$ X 3IN) PURSE

Materials

19 x 26.5cm (7$^1/_2$ x 10$^3/_8$in) #18 mesh canvas
(this allows for a 4cm (1$^1/_2$in) margin all the
way around the design)
No. 22 tapestry needle
23cm (¹/₄yd) lining fabric
Three small black snap fasteners
It's Polite to Point® Heirloom Quality
Needleart Wool in the colours listed below

Flap

Back

Front

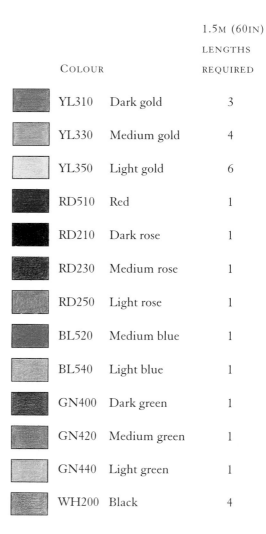

Colour			1.5M (60IN) LENGTHS REQUIRED
	YL310	Dark gold	3
	YL330	Medium gold	4
	YL350	Light gold	6
	RD510	Red	1
	RD210	Dark rose	1
	RD230	Medium rose	1
	RD250	Light rose	1
	BL520	Medium blue	1
	BL540	Light blue	1
	GN400	Dark green	1
	GN420	Medium green	1
	GN440	Light green	1
	WH200	Black	4

Use one of the three plies at a time. For general
stitching instructions and conversions for other mesh
sizes, see Basic Techniques, page 11.

Making the Evening Bag

Follow the chart on page 63 to work the evening bag design with one ply of the three-ply yarn; block the needlepoint (see page 120). Cut out a piece of lining fabric the same size as the canvas. Pin the needlepoint to the lining, right sides together. Beginning at the inside corner of the curve where the front and side join, sew around the curve and all the way around the very edge of the needlepoint, leaving the top of the bag front open for turning. Try to produce a smoothly rounded seam along the top of the sides.

Trim the seam allowances to just 6mm (1/4in). Clip off the seam allowance diagonally at the outside corners and snip almost to the inside corners. Snip into the seam allowance at curves every 6mm (1/4in).

Turn the bag out and slip stitch the opening closed. Press from the lining side. Crease the folds to form the bag using the tip of the iron. Hand-stitch each side section to the bottom of the purse, then to the back of the purse, continuing up around the top of the side where it curves. Stop stitching at the middle of the curve. Stitch one part of the Velcro spots to the lattice purse front, using five spots placed in every other diamond in a row of nine diamonds across. Then attach the other parts of the spots to the inside of the front flap to correspond. Finally, stitch the ends of your cord to the top of the sides for the strap – check that the length of the cord strap is satisfactory before stitching it firmly in place.

Working with Multi-Fibres

I restitched the evening bag and purse with a variety of fibres – silk ribbons, floss, metallics and nylon tubing with a metallic through the centre. Because these threads were all used in the form in which they came, not separated into plies, it took three times as much fibre as Persian wool. To determine how much you will need to buy, multiply the total wool requirements by three, then divide this by the length in which the skein or card is available.

Speciality fibres can be expensive, so try using stranded cotton (floss) for most of the colours and select just a few metallics for dazzling highlights. Although the bag is lovely, I found that the expensive silk ribbons really did not produce an appreciable difference, so I suggest you experiment – you might discover, as I did, that a less expensive fibre will create the same look.

However, when I purchase metallics or silks for highlights, I usually prefer the best, as with my wools. I invest in the best fibres available so that my work will outlive my generation and become an heirloom.

EVENING BAG

STITCH COUNT: 184 x 261
FINISHED STITCHED SIZE:
APPROXIMATELY 26.5 x 37CM (10³/₈ x 14¹/₂IN) FOR A
15 x 11.5 x 5CM (6 x 4¹/₂ x 2IN) BAG

Materials

*34 x 44.5cm (13³/₈ x 17¹/₂in) #18 mesh canvas
(this allows for a 4cm (1¹/₂in) margin all the
way around the design)
No. 22 tapestry needle
34cm (³/₈yd) lining fabric
Cord the finished length plus 15cm (6in)
Five black 12mm (¹/₂in) Velcro light-duty spots
It's Polite to Point® Heirloom Quality
Needleart Wool in the colours listed below*

Colour			1.5M (60IN) LENGTHS REQUIRED
	YL310	Dark gold	4
	YL330	Medium gold	10
	YL350	Light gold	17
	RD510	Red	1
	RD210	Dark rose	1
	RD230	Medium rose	1
	RD250	Light rose	1
	BL520	Medium blue	1
	BL540	Light blue	1
	GN400	Dark green	4
	GN420	Medium green	4
	GN440	Light green	3
	WH200	Black	21
	WH620	Cream	2

Use one of the three plies at a time. For general stitching instructions and conversions for other mesh sizes, see Basic Techniques, page 11.

Front

Base

Back

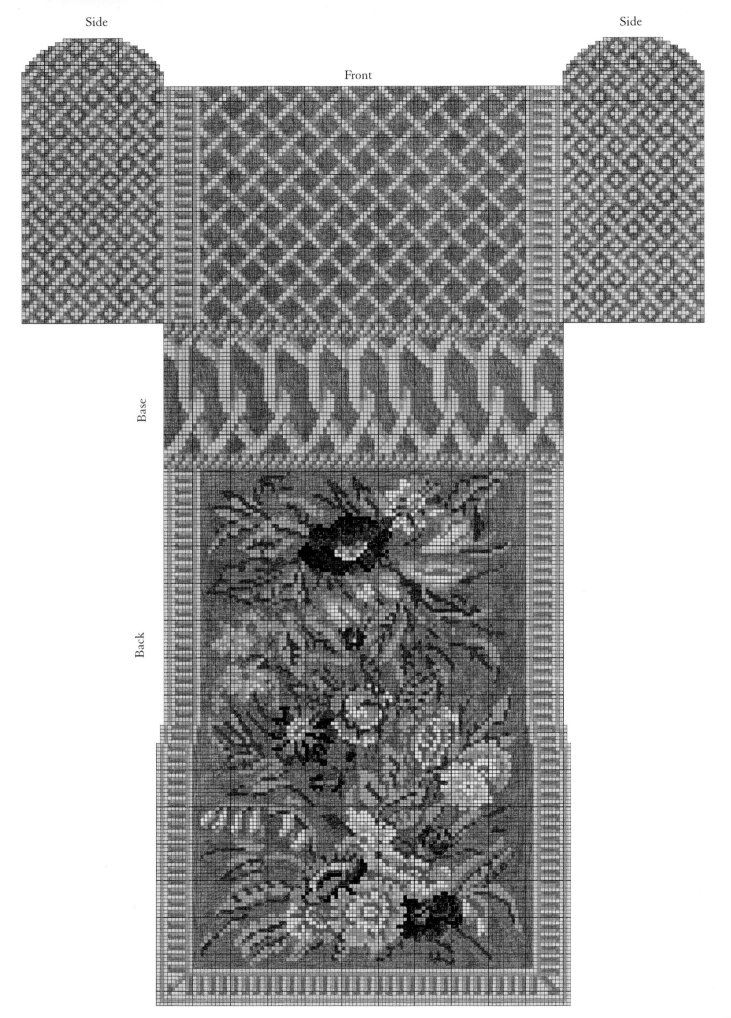

Flap

Cornucopias

A HANDSOME PRINTED COTTON FABRIC (1775-1800) IN WINTERTHUR'S TEXTILE ARCHIVES WAS THE INSPIRATION FOR THE NEEDLEWORK PATTERNS IN THIS CHAPTER. ACORNS, UNDULATING VINES AND LAVISH CORNUCOPIAS OVERFLOWING WITH FLOWERS AND FRUITS BRING BEAUTY TO ANY ROOM.

While working at Winterthur, I was particularly drawn to an unusual rectangular fragment of cloth. The rich deep-red print on a neutral background stopped me in my tracks. Colour, striped symmetries and the interplay of forms were what I noticed first. Upon closer inspection I realized that a multitude of stunning details offered unlimited possibilities for design adaptation.

Though the origin of the fabric is not documented, the lush design, overall richness of pattern and naturalistic rendering of elements was typical of English textiles between 1775 and 1800. The remnant had been printed with hand-engraved copperplates, a technique related to etching, which enjoyed a brief period of popularity in the second half of the eighteenth century.

In 1752, at the Drumcondra print-works outside Dublin, Francis Nixon introduced copperplate printing and it was initiated soon after in England. By the early 1760s, several English factories in the London area, including Robert Jones of Old Ford and the firm of Bromley Hall in Middlesex, England, were producing top-quality copperplate prints. Many of these fabrics, among the finest of all English printed textiles, were exported to the rapidly expanding American Colonies.

The copperplate printing procedure begins with master artists who engrave fine images on flat copper plates that are then rubbed with printing dye. Next, the dye is wiped off the surface, remaining only in the incised lines of the engraving. Cloth is then laid over the plate and extreme pressure is applied with a mechanical press, transferring the design to the cloth. Finally, the cloth is shifted and the process repeated. The main limitation of the process was that the fabrics could be produced only in one colour. It was difficult to overprint with a second colour because the detailed engraving made it almost impossible to match up a second image to the first. The basic dyestuff used was madder, which produced a whole range of colours, including pinks, reds, purples or black. China blue, which required a laborious and chemically sophisticated series of dyeing operations using indigo, was also popular.

The opulence of a late eighteenth-century fabric is captured in the gold and teal designs shown here. I worked the gold version a second time in decorative embroidery stitches (front).

In earlier fabric printing methods, the size of motifs had been governed by the size of printing-block that could be managed comfortably by hand. However, the first copperplates were large, measuring up to 1m (3ft) square. This enabled the designer to work with large-scale patterns. With repeats up to 1m (3ft) long, the fabrics were quite suitable for furnishings.

Although the initial engraving of copperplates was time-consuming and therefore expensive, their large size made more naturalistic rendering of larger-scale patterns possible. The finer etching allowed for more subtle effects in light and shading than could be achieved with earlier block-printing. With this innovative technology, new styles of patterns evolved. Designers turned to paintings, prints and book illustrations for inspiration. They copied details, sometimes from a great variety of sources, then reassembled the motifs to form new compositions. The fabric patterns which developed included a wide range of floral and bird patterns, exotic designs, especially chinoiseries, pastoral and theatrical scenes and episodes from classical mythology or recent history.

The origin of the cornucopia motif, the inspiration for this chapter's projects, is rooted in Greek mythology. When the Titan Kronos ruled the universe, he feared he would be overthrown by one of his children, so he ate them, but his wife, Rhea, hid his last born son, Zeus, in a cave on the island of Crete. A tribe of nymphs protected Zeus and fed him goat's milk. When the grateful Zeus grew up, he gave the goat's horn to the nymphs and promised that it would be a perpetual source of milk and honey, the ambrosia of the gods. The horn of plenty, the cornucopia, with its classical ancestry and symbolism of a bountiful harvest, is a recurring textile motif.

This copperplate-printed cotton textile fragment was made between 1775 and 1800, probably in England.

Development of Copperplate Printing

Surviving pattern-books from English eighteenth-century copperplate printers show that the Dublin and London printers enjoyed a virtual monopoly of copperplate printing for almost a quarter of a century. Then, in the 1770s, Christoph Philipp Oberkampf, considered the father of French textile printing, adopted the technique. He set up his factory at Jouy-en-Josas outside Paris and it became one of the most famous and successful print-works in France.

Between 1760 and 1800 the copperplate printing technique was used to produce some of the finest printed textiles that survive today. Especially popular were those French and British monochrome pictorial prints of the late eighteenth century, commonly called toiles de Jouy. Though it was the British who pioneered the copperplate printing process which revolutionized the textile industry, we recognize the French as the leaders in design and they sustain that reputation today.

Working with Multi-stitches

I worked the gold cornucopia a second time using a variety of creative embroidery stitches. This didn't require any more wool than the standard tent-stitch version. Refer to Basic Techniques, page 11, for general instructions on working with multi-stitches. Here are details of the stitches I used and the number of plies:

Bullion – curly shoots extending from the grape vine; 2-ply.

Outline – green grape vines; 2-ply.

Chain – vertical white stripes on the maroon ribbons; 2-ply.

Straight – ornaments on the outer sections of the maroon ribbons, ornaments on the central section of the teal ribbon, right-hand red grapes, three left-hand flowers; 2-ply.

French knot – ornaments on the outer sections and the centres of the central ornaments on the teal ribbon, centres of the outer ornaments of the maroon ribbons, centres of the five flowers at the top of the cornucopia; 2-ply.

Cross with a back stitch – orange fruit; 1-ply.

Mosaic – background; 2-ply.

Couching – cornucopia; 2-ply for the main lines and 1-ply for the anchoring stitches.

Making the Cornucopia Rug

I devised the rug design from a combination of the two cornucopia patterns. Working on a #10 mesh canvas, I stitched the entire square gold cornucopia pattern first. Then I added 21 more rows of white stitches, to the left and right, beyond the original square design and placed here the two outer ribbons from the teal cornucopia pattern. There are a total of 34 white stitches between the acorn-entwined burgundy ribbon and the grape-leaf-entwined teal ribbon. I completed a band of background 30 stitches wide, beyond both outer teal ribbons. The finished needlepoint is 89 x 48cm (35 x 19in).

You will need a 96.5 x 56cm (38 x 22in) rectangle of #10 mesh canvas (this allows for a 4cm (1 1/2in) margin all the way around the design); 70cm (3/4yd) of 114cm (45in) wide heavyweight backing fabric; 3.2m (31/2yd) of trim. Work the rug as described above with a No. 18 tapestry needle, referring to the charts on pages 68-71. Use all three plies at a time. You will need the following 1.5m (60in) lengths of wool (refer to the charts for colour numbers): 76 of dark teal; 16 of medium teal; 12 of light teal; 27 of dark green; 24 of medium green; 10 of light green; 56 of dark maroon; 6 of medium rose; 6 of light rose; 3 of pale pink; 31 of medium rusty brown; 33 of orange gold; 8 of light peach; 304 of ivory.

When you have finished the needlepoint, stitch it to the backing with right sides facing, leaving a band of bare canvas showing all round which is one thread narrower than the width of your trim. Leave a gap to turn through in one edge and leave the corners open by at least the width of the trim. Turn the rug right-sides out and slip stitch the opening closed. Slip stitch the trim to the top and bottom edges of the rug, slipping the ends into the corner gaps. Next slip stitch the trim to the remaining edges, again tucking it in at the corners. Secure the corners with slip stitches. Turn the rug over and tack the backing to the underside of the needlepoint at intervals to prevent it slipping.

I worked this beautiful rug on #10 mesh canvas, using the gold cornucopia design as the centrepiece and adding elements from the teal version to extend it.

GOLD CORNUCOPIA

STITCH COUNT: 198 x 195

FINISHED STITCHED SIZE: APPROXIMATELY 35.5 x 35.5CM (14 x 14IN)

Materials

43.5 x 43.5cm (17 x 17in) #14 mesh canvas (this allows for a 4cm (1¹/₂in)
margin all the way around the design)

No. 22 tapestry needle

It's Polite to Point® Heirloom Quality Needleart Wool in the colours listed below

	Colour		1.5M (60IN) LENGTHS REQUIRED
	BL200	Dark teal	18
	BL220	Medium teal	8
	BL240	Light teal	6
	GN000	Dark green	6
	GN030	Medium green	7
	GN140	Light green	2
	RD190	Dark maroon	27
	RD270	Medium rose	3
	RD330	Light rose	3
	RD460	Pale pink	2
	OR710	Medium rusty brown	8
	YL230	Orange gold	9
	OR040	Light peach	3
	WH620	Ivory	68

Use two of the three plies at a time. For general stitching instructions and
conversions for other mesh sizes, see Basic Techniques, page 11.

Multi-stitch Alternative

I restitched the gold cornucopia in a variety of creative embroidery stitches. You can use
your own choice of stitches or follow mine, as given on page 66.

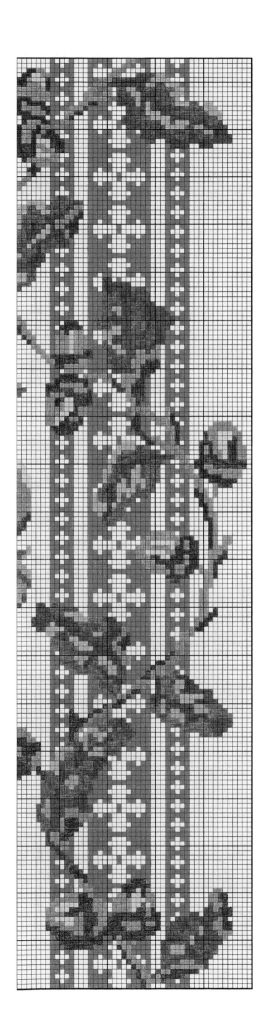

TEAL CORNUCOPIA

STITCH COUNT: 198 x 195

FINISHED STITCHED SIZE: APPROXIMATELY 35.5 x 35.5CM (14 x 14IN)

Materials

43.5 x 43.5cm (17 x 17in) #14 mesh canvas (this allows for a 4cm (1¹/2in)
margin all the way around the design)
No. 22 tapestry needle
It's Polite to Point® Heirloom Quality Needleart Wool in the colours listed below

	Colour		1.5M (60IN) LENGTHS REQUIRED
	BL200	Dark teal	20
	BL220	Medium teal	5
	BL240	Light teal	4
	GN000	Dark green	10
	GN030	Medium green	9
	GN140	Light green	5
	RD190	Dark maroon	9
	RD270	Medium rose	3
	RD330	Light rose	4
	RD460	Pale pink	3
	OR710	Medium rusty brown	10
	YL230	Orange gold	10
	OR040	Light peach	3
	WH620	Ivory	75

Use two of the three plies at a time. For general stitching instructions and
conversions for other mesh sizes, see Basic Techniques, page 11.

Hill & Dale

PASTORAL SCENES OF DELIGHTFUL CREATURES, A SHEPHERD AND HUNTSMAN, AND
FANCIFUL FLOWERS SET ON A BACKGROUND OF ROLLING HILLS AND DALES ADORN
THE FOLLOWING PROJECTS. I ADAPTED THE DESIGNS FROM AN ELABORATE TWELVE-
PIECE SET OF CREWEL AND SILK EMBROIDERED HANGINGS, PROBABLY MADE IN
ENGLAND BETWEEN 1680 AND 1740.

Du Pont organized the rooms at Winterthur around a domestic activity and period in history. His Patuxent bedroom captivated me during
one of my first trips to Winterthur, revealing the British influence on
life in early America.

During the seventeenth and eighteenth centuries, as they gained a permanent
foothold in America, the new settlers arrived with some of their favourite furniture, curtains, bed hangings and embroideries. As they were primarily
Englishmen, the early Colonists had a preference for English upholstery and furnishings. They were striving to adapt long-familiar ways to the demands of a
bewildering new land, so they set about shaping the wilderness as best they could
with the elaborations of their former residences. The Patuxent room illustrates
this with its black transfer-printed tea set made in Worcester, England. The elaborate set of bed hangings, also British, demonstrates the Colonists' affection for
the bright embroideries that had graced their earlier homes.

During the early Colonial period, the master bed was commonly located in
the parlour and seen by all visitors. It was usually the most important piece of furniture in the house and, when means were available, the most lavishly decorated. It was not the ornate carving, but rather the draping of elegant fabric that represented the owner's status and wealth. A complete set of bed furniture for a four-
poster bed consisted of valances, headcloth, bedspread, and four side curtains
wide and long enough to enclose the bed.

In monetary terms, textiles were the largest commodity imported into the
Colonies, and estate inventories from that period show large expenditures for bed
furnishings. The choice between imports or homespun fabrics depended on
access to sources of supply and the ability to pay for costly imports. Those in
modest circumstances had to rely largely on their own resources, making fabrics
from scratch, while affluent citizens of seaport communities were probably content with nothing less than the latest and best from England.

Embroideries were also treasures in the true sense of the word and were
accorded the same respect reserved for precious belongings. Creating them
required hard-learned skills, time, patience and materials not always easy to

Following the English pastoral tradition, the shepherd (left) and piper (right)
cushions nevertheless exhibit the eighteenth-century American preference for
simple design containing flora and fauna that could be found in the New World.

In the eighteenth century, people still frequently used bedrooms, like the Patuxent room, for the informal entertaining of guests.

come by. Months, even years, of labour often went into some of the larger, more elaborate works. Consequently, bequeathing embroideries was seldom left to chance, and great care was taken to place them where they would be appreciated and well cared for.

Because the bed was one of the most valued possessions, it was the most usual article decorated with the beloved crewel embroidery. This needleart is worked on most types of fabric in a firm, two-ply variety of wool called 'crewel', from which it draws its name. The varied design possibilities afforded by the colourful crewels made them extremely appealing for the challenging and expensive task of decorating the bed.

Among the early Colonists the most popular crewel designs followed the English tradition of arboreal and floral motifs. After a time, as the Colonial American needlewoman's crewel work evolved, she developed somewhat simpler lines. She preferred balanced patterns that led the eye along flowing lines to discover one element after another. Though a motif was rarely repeated, there was still an overall effect of design unity. Unicorns, griffins and other imaginary or wild beasts found in English works did not appear to interest the Colonists. They favoured gentler, less fanciful animals and drew upon the local scene for new inspiration. They transformed the animals, flowers and trees found in English and East Indian designs into those that were an integral part of American life, such as sheep, chickens, wild grapes and pine trees.

Gradually, a modified American style emerged that conveyed a feeling of spaciousness and independence. Perhaps this was a reflection of an environment where freedom of choice and open country, as far as the eye could see, were common. The Patuxent room bed hangings, with their perfect technique and balanced proportions, indicate a professional hand and were most likely done in an English workroom. Yet they seem to blend the American preferences for flowing lines and ordinary animals with the repeat motif and exacting technique more customary of England.

By the late eighteenth century, improvements in home heating reduced bed hangings to more decorative functions and by the end of the century, when furniture styles changed, they were no longer in vogue. Today, few complete sets of crewel bed hangings survive because as they began to wear out, their good parts were often cut out and used in other pieces. In a similar fashion, I have picked out some of my favourite elements from the Patuxent room bed hangings design and pieced them together into two square patterns. I have also displayed the piper design in an additional colourway, the palette selected to match a wallpaper I like. You can find information about how you can adapt patterns to match your personal preferences in the Basic Techniques section, page 11.

The piper cushion, stitched in the alternative colourway, is set off perfectly by a thick gold fringe.

PIPER

STITCH COUNT: 199 X 202
FINISHED STITCHED SIZE: APPROXIMATELY 35.5 X 35.5CM (14 X 14IN)

Materials

43.5 x 43.5cm (17 x 17in) #14 mesh canvas (this allows for a
4cm (1½in) margin all the way around the design)
No. 22 tapestry needle
It's Polite to Point® Heirloom Quality Needleart Wool in the colours listed below

	COLOUR		ALTERNATIVE COLOURWAY		1.5M (60IN) LENGTHS REQUIRED
	WH200	Black	WH200	Black	3
	BR320	Dark brown	BR240	Dark brown gold	7
	BR340	Medium brown	YL420	Medium gold	7
	BR360	Light brown	YL440	Light gold	4
	RD310	Dark rose	OR710	Dark brick rose	2
	RD320	Medium pink rose	OR730	Medium brick rose	4
	RD340	Light pink rose	OR750	Light brick rose	4
	YL410	Dark gold	BL130	Medium blue	4
	YL440	Light gold	BL150	Light blue	14
	GN760	Medium blue green	GN260	Medium true green	18
	GN050	Light green	GN130	Light yellow green	9
	BL000	Dark blue	GN600	Dark hunter green	13
	BL020	Medium blue	GN010	Medium olive green	12
	BL040	Light blue	GN760	Light teal green	2
	WH620	Ivory	WH630	Cream	53

Use two of the three plies at a time. For general stitching instructions and
conversions for other mesh sizes, see Basic Techniques, page 11.

Alternative Colourway

I restitched the piper in another colourway to complement a wallpaper I like. The shift in
colours and the addition of an opulent trim changed the look to one of more sophisticated ele-
gance. Simply convert the chart by replacing the wool shades with the alternative colourway.

SHEPHERD

STITCH COUNT: 199 X 202

FINISHED STITCHED SIZE: APPROXIMATELY 35.5 X 35.5CM (14 X 14IN)

Materials

43.5 x 43.5cm (17 x 17in) #14 mesh canvas (this allows for a

4cm (1¹/2in) margin all the way around the design)

No. 22 tapestry needle

It's Polite to Point® Heirloom Quality Needleart Wool in the colours listed below

	COLOUR		1.5M (60IN) LENGTHS REQUIRED
	WH200	Black	4
	BR320	Dark brown	6
	BR340	Medium brown	15
	BR360	Light brown	8
	RD310	Dark rose	1
	RD320	Medium pink rose	4
	RD340	Light pink rose	3
	YL410	Dark gold	6
	YL440	Light gold	10
	GN760	Medium blue green	20
	GN050	Light green	9
	BL000	Dark blue	14
	BL020	Medium blue	14
	BL040	Light blue	3
	WH620	Ivory	39

Use two of the three plies at a time. For general stitching instructions and
conversions for other mesh sizes, see Basic Techniques, page 11.

Victorian Country Garden Bouquets

CAPTURE THE VICTORIAN LOVE OF FLORALS, RICH COLOUR AND PATTERN WITH THESE TWO DESIGNS IN TWO COLOURWAYS. MAKE THEM INTO CUSHIONS OR COVER A FOOTSTOOL, OR DEVISE YOUR OWN WAY OF SHOWING THEM OFF.

Textiles played a vital role in the lives of American Colonists and were the largest imported commodity. They were more highly prized than anything else, except land, buildings and, in rare instances, wrought silver. Commerce was closely linked with fashion, and imports powerfully influenced textile use throughout the seventeenth, eighteenth and nineteenth centuries in America. Winterthur's textile collections reveal that Americans followed European, especially English and French, upholstery and furnishing styles.

By the time Queen Victoria ascended the throne in 1837, an unending variety of lush, naturalistic flower designs had emerged in textiles and needlework. Many flower motifs, modelled on paintings and engravings of the time, depicted detailed and accurate representations of numerous flowers. The country-garden florals interpreted for my designs reflect typically extravagant Victorian fashion. Such lavish patterns demanded a wide range of colour harmonies, so they were block-printed by hand well after technology made machine printing possible.

Block-printing is the earliest form of textile printing and was used in India as early as the fourth century B.C. By the late Middle Ages, block-printing was an established trade in Europe, particularly in Italy and Germany. In 1676 William Sherwin of West Ham, near London, probably the first calico printer in England to use the fast-dye technique, obtained a patent 'for a new way for printing and stayning' calico.

By 1700 the English block-printing industry was well-established around London along the tributaries of the River Thames, wherever fresh, clear water was plentiful for the dyeing and clearing (washing) processes, and it became very lucrative during the eighteenth and early nineteenth centuries. The United States produced little commercial block-printing through the first three-quarters of the eighteenth century while imports were abundant, but by 1774 the John Hewson and Bedwell & Walters printworks were both operating near Philadelphia.

These designs reflect the British love of gardens and demonstrate that flower motifs never go out of style. Choose between the exotic tulips (top) or luscious lilies (centre) in their original colourway, or work the alternative versions for cushions or a footstool (below and page 19).

Block Printing Technique

For block printing, small, easily manipulated blocks are carved for each colour. The cloth is stretched tight on a long padded table and the printer presses the block face against a dye-saturated wooden sieve and sets the block on the stretched cloth. With a hefty blow with a wooden mallet to the back of the block, he transfers the carved image onto the fabric. After every stroke of the mallet, the printer moves the block to the next undyed space on the cloth, carefully aligning the pattern. Repeating this process with a separate block and a different dye for each colour creates a broad range of colours.

In 1783 Scotsman Thomas Bell invented the engraved metal-roller-printer and by the mid-nineteenth century the fabric-printing industry was primarily mechanized. Today, block printing is largely obsolete, though it is still used on a limited scale for expensive home-furnishing fabrics.

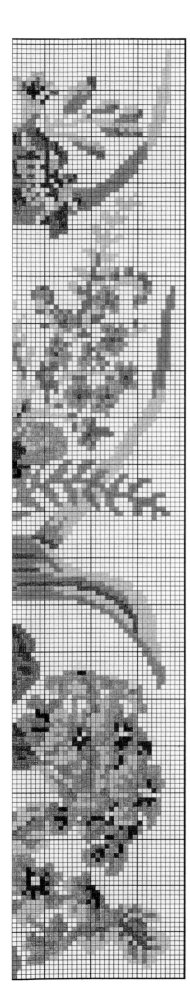

TULIPS

STITCH COUNT: 199 X 201

FINISHED STITCHED SIZE: APPROXIMATELY 35.5 X 35.5CM (14 X 14IN)

Materials

43.5 x 43.5cm (17 x 17in) #14 mesh canvas (this allows for a
4cm (1¹/2in) margin all the way around the design)
No. 22 tapestry needle
It's Polite to Point® Heirloom Quality Needleart Wool in the colours listed below

	Colour		1.5M (60IN) LENGTHS REQUIRED		Colour		1.5M (60IN) LENGTHS REQUIRED
	BL210	Dark teal	21		RD000	Darkest purple maroon	5
	BL230	Medium teal	18		RD260	Dark rose	7
	BL790	Dark blue	3		RD320	Medium pink rose	7
	BL540	Light blue	3		RD340	Light pink rose	2
	GN570	Medium golden green	2		OR740	Light peach	3
	GN420	Medium khaki green	5		BR660	Dark brown	11
	YL220	Dark rust gold	6		BR360	Light brown	6
	YL240	Medium gold	5		WH600	Ivory	5
	YL270	Light yellow	4		BR750	Creamy beige	62

Use two of the three plies at a time. For general stitching instructions and
conversions for other mesh sizes, see Basic Techniques, page 11. To work this tapestry
to cover a footstool you may need to adjust the canvas mesh size so the design fits.

Alternative Colourway

I repeated the tulips with a dark brown background shade, while retaining the palette from the light background version, altering only the white. Use five lengths of WH630, a slightly creamier white, to replace WH600 Ivory. Replace BR750 Creamy beige with BR660 Dark brown. You will need a total of 73 lengths of BR660, the amount within the design (11 lengths) added to the background (62 lengths).

LILIES

STITCH COUNT: 199 x 201

FINISHED STITCHED SIZE: APPROXIMATELY 35.5 x 35.5cm (14 x 14in)

Materials

43.5 x 43.5cm (17 x 17in) #14 mesh canvas (this allows for a 4cm (1¹/2in)
margin all the way around the design)
No. 22 tapestry needle
It's Polite to Point® Heirloom Quality Needleart Wool in the colours listed below

	COLOUR		1.5M (60IN) LENGTHS REQUIRED		COLOUR		1.5M (60IN) LENGTHS REQUIRED
	BL210	Dark teal	17		RD000	Darkest purple maroon	7
	BL230	Medium teal	22		RD260	Dark rose	6
	BL790	Dark blue	4		RD320	Medium pink rose	9
	BL540	Light blue	4		RD340	Light pink rose	5
	GN570	Medium golden green	1		OR740	Light peach	3
	GN420	Medium khaki green	4		BR660	Dark brown	9
	YL220	Dark rust gold	2		BR360	Light brown	11
	YL240	Medium gold	2		WH600	Ivory	8
	YL270	Light yellow	2		BR750	Creamy beige	60

Use two of the three plies at a time. For general stitching instructions and
conversions for other mesh sizes, see Basic Techniques, page 11. To work this
tapestry to cover a footstool you may need to adjust the canvas mesh size so
the design fits.

Alternative Colourway

I repeated the lilies with a dark brown background shade, while retaining the palette
from the light background version, altering only the white. Use eight lengths of WH630,
a slightly creamier white, to replace WH600 Ivory. Replace BR750 Creamy beige with
BR660 Dark brown. You will need a total of 69 lengths of BR660, the amount within the
design (9 lengths) added to the background (60 lengths).

Luscious Fruits

VOLUMES OF NINETEENTH-CENTURY BOTANICAL BOOKS IN WINTERTHUR'S RARE BOOK COLLECTION INSPIRED THESE LUSCIOUS FRUIT DESIGNS. THE BOOKS' EXTRAVAGANT ILLUSTRATIONS WERE FREQUENTLY REPRODUCED BY YOUNG WOMEN IN THEIR EMBROIDERY.

Nature, especially horticulture, was an important science in the nineteenth century. Volumes such as George Brookshaw's *Pomona Britannica* (London, 1817), John Lindley's *Pomologia Britannica* (London, 1841), H. Whittock's *The Art of Drawing Flowers, Fruits and Shells* (London, 1829) and C.V. Hovey's *Fruits of America* (Boston, 1852) contain accurate and lavish illustrations. The fruit tree, plants and other images of nature provided scientific information, but were equally appreciated for their beauty. The richly hand-coloured drawings were often framed by home decorators or reproduced by young women in their handiwork, as I have done for these fruit cushions and coasters.

I discovered the botanical books listed above in the Winterthur library's Rare Book Collection. Among the hundreds of items in the library's botanical holdings, images range from scientific to decorative and the artists from well-known to amateur. Of course, I selected my favourite images from the collection to create the following projects.

The Rare Book Collection contains volumes of rare American and European imprints. The holdings include: architecture and design pattern books; American and British manufacturers' and retailers' trade catalogues; descriptions of craft techniques; periodicals that promote or describe life-styles; and city directories and guidebooks. This collection offers limitless insights into European practices that influenced American taste and design.

The Collection is just one division of the Winterthur library. Established in 1951 with material collected by Henry F. du Pont, the library today is one of the world's most comprehensive resources for the study of American art, material culture and history before 1914. It is also the repository of du Pont's papers, many of which document his collecting, garden designs and plans for Winterthur. More than 70,000 bound volumes and about 500,000 manuscripts, pamphlets, advertising ephemera, trade catalogues, books of textile swatches, diaries, photographs and slides are available for use by scholars and the general public.

These colourful cushions are positively mouth-watering. Both the large melon design (right) and large pineapple (top left) mingle with other delicious fruits including grapes, star fruit, plums and strawberries. The set of four coasters (below left) features peaches, pears, gooseberries and grapes. Against their black backgrounds the colours of the fruits seem to glow, but you could choose a background colour to match a room scheme.

*These stunning illustrations of peaches and strawberries (*Pomologia Britannica *by John Lindley) are typical of the high-quality illustrations which inspired the designs in this chapter.*

Though the variety of the Collection is almost limitless, the strength of the library's collections is in three areas: materials that describe the design, production, marketing and use of American domestic objects and many of their foreign models and antecedents; materials that record and illustrate American art and architecture; and materials that document everyday life in America from its beginnings to the twentieth century.

Winterthur considers these manuscripts, photographs, books and magazines as much cultural artefacts as research tools. Thus, the library is crucial to Winterthur's mission to be a centre for the study of American culture. Maintaining it is more than simply an issue of stewardship. The library staff continually seeks to expand the varied collections and make the resources even more accessible to researchers.

The vast resources of the library continually challenge and enthrall me. It was here that I discovered the exquisite botanical books from which I adapted the coasters and cushions. It is easy to imagine, with his passion for gardening and scientific farming, that Henry F. du Pont would have appreciated the bounty represented in these vibrant designs. As a young man he studied practical horticulture at Harvard's Bussey Institution. Following his return to Winterthur in 1902, he conducted a series of landscape design experiments and colour studies that formed the basis for the naturalistic approach and imaginative colour combinations apparent in the garden today. I have attempted to capture in the colour and detail of my botanical interpretations the heart and vision of a man who fashioned one of America's most beautiful gardens.

Making the Coasters

I have found that a very uncomplicated method of finishing coasters precludes having to refinish them at a later date. Often, when cardboard or cork is inserted, after long use they will begin to disintegrate. So, very simply, I back my coasters with a sturdy backing fabric.

Stitch the coasters to the backing with right sides facing. Starting on the lower left edge of each coaster, machine-stitch all the way around the needlepoint, being careful to catch only the very edge of the outermost row of stitches. Leave a 6.5cm (2¹/₂in) opening along the bottom edge for turning. Clip the corners diagonally across the seam allowance, close to the seam, then turn the coaster right-sides out. Slip stitch the gap closed, then press the seams flat from the backing side.

Making the Cushions

Stitch the designs for the cushions following your chosen chart. To make each small cushion you will need about 1.10m (1¹/₄yd) of trim and a 33cm (13in) square of backing fabric. For each of the larger cushions you will need about 1.6m (1³/₄yd) of trim and a 43cm (17in) square of backing fabric. Block the design and finish it knife-edge style (see page 122) attaching the trim before or after assembly depending on its type (see page 122).

A fresh pineapple (left) and ripe melon (right) seem to burst forth, out of their cushions, demanding attention.

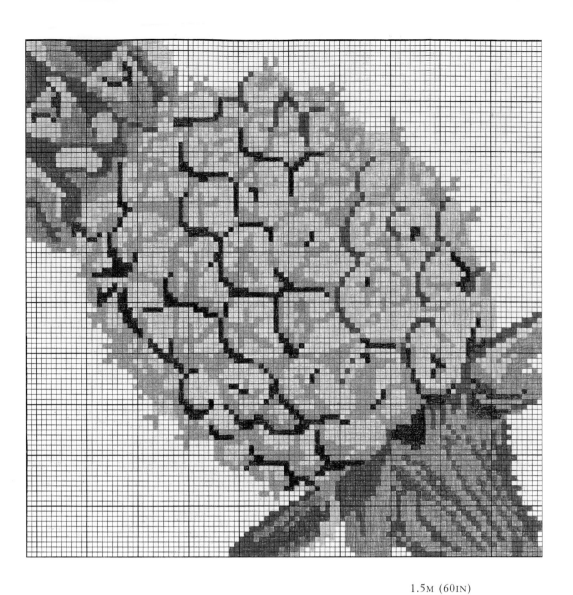

SMALL PINEAPPLE

STITCH COUNT: 102 X 103
FINISHED STITCHED SIZE:
APPROXIMATELY 25.5 X 25.5CM (10 X 10IN)

Materials

33 x 33cm (13 x 13in) #10 mesh canvas (this
allows for a 4cm (1¹/₂in) margin all the way
around the design)
No. 18 tapestry needle
It's Polite to Point® Heirloom Quality
Needleart Wool in the colours listed right

	COLOUR		1.5M (60IN) LENGTHS REQUIRED
	GN610	Dark blue green	8
	GN630	Medium blue green	7
	GN650	Light blue green	6
	GN100	Dark moss green	2
	GN120	Medium moss green	3
	YL010	Bright gold	13
	YL030	Medium golden yellow	23
	PP220	Medium reddish purple	7
	PP130	Medium blue purple	1
	BL790	Teal blue background	28

Use all three plies at a time. For general stitching instructions and
conversions for other mesh sizes, see Basic Techniques, page 11.

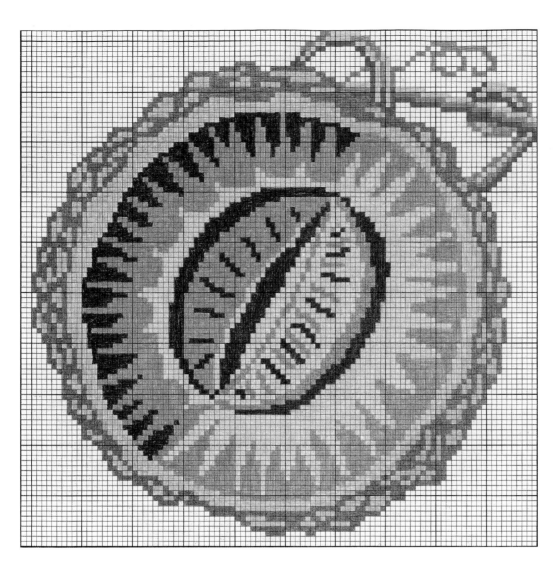

SMALL MELON

STITCH COUNT: 102 X 102
FINISHED STITCHED SIZE:
APPROXIMATELY 25.5 X 25.5CM (10 X 10IN)

Materials

*33 x 33cm (13 x 13in) #10 mesh canvas (this
allows for a 4cm (1¹/₂in) margin all the way
around the design)*
No. 18 tapestry needle
*It's Polite to Point® Heirloom Quality
Needleart Wool in the colours listed right*

	COLOUR		1.5M (60IN) LENGTHS REQUIRED
	GN610	Dark blue green	2
	GN630	Medium blue green	2
	GN650	Light blue green	5
	GN100	Dark moss green	8
	GN140	Light moss green	1
	OR420	Bright orange red	9
	OR440	Medium salmon	17
	OR460	Light salmon	12
	YL030	Medium golden yellow	6
	BL790	Teal blue background	25

*Use all three plies at a time. For general stitching instructions and
conversions for other mesh sizes, see Basic Techniques, page 11.*

COASTER SET

STITCH COUNT: 58 X 59

FINISHED STITCHED SIZE: APPROXIMATELY 10 X 10CM (4 X 4IN)

Materials

33 x 33cm (13 x 13in) #14 mesh canvas (this allows for a 4cm (1¹/₂in) margin all
the way around the design with 5cm (2in) separating the coasters)
No. 22 tapestry needle
23cm (¹/₄yd) black upholstery-weight backing fabric
It's Polite to Point® Heirloom Quality Needleart Wool in the colours listed below

	COLOUR		1.5M (60IN) LENGTHS REQUIRED
	RD190	Dark rose	3
	RD310	Medium rose	4
	OR640	Medium peach	4
	YL260	Dark yellow	3
	YL040	Light yellow	1
	BL740	Dark blue	5
	BL610	Medium blue	4
	BL640	Light blue	2
	GN000	Dark green	4
	GN120	Medium green	5
	GN940	Light green	3
	BR320	Dark brown	2
	BR350	Medium brown	2
	WH200	Black	21

Use two of the three plies at a time. For general stitching instructions and
conversions for other mesh sizes, see Basic Techniques, page 11.

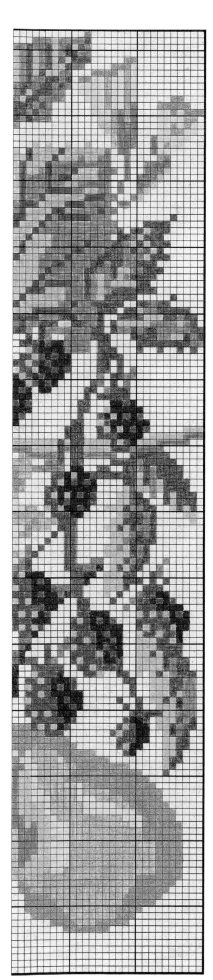

LARGE MELON

STITCH COUNT: 143 X 143

FINISHED STITCHED SIZE: APPROXIMATELY 35.5 X 35.5CM (14 X 14IN)

Materials

43.5 x 43.5cm (17 x 17in) #10 mesh canvas (this allows for a 4cm (1¹/2in)
margin all the way around the design)
No. 18 tapestry needle
It's Polite to Point® Heirloom Quality Needleart Wool in the colours listed below

COLOUR		1.5M (60IN) LENGTHS REQUIRED	COLOUR		1.5M (60IN) LENGTHS REQUIRED
GN610	Dark blue green	4	YL030	Medium golden yellow	13
GN630	Medium blue green	8	YL040	Light golden yellow	6
GN650	Light blue green	8	PP110	Dark blue purple	4
GN100	Dark moss green	18	PP130	Medium blue purple	1
GN120	Medium moss green	11	PP220	Medium reddish purple	5
GN140	Light moss green	5	PP440	Light lavender blue	1
GN930	Medium yellow green	8	RD410	Bright pink red	4
GN950	Light yellow green	8	RD440	Medium pink	4
OR420	Bright orange red	10	RD460	Light pink	2
OR440	Medium salmon	17	BR010	Dark brown	1
OR460	Light salmon	13	BR030	Medium brown	3
YL010	Bright gold	4	BL790	Teal blue background	35

Use all three plies at a time. For general stitching instructions and conversions
for other mesh sizes, see Basic Techniques, page 11.

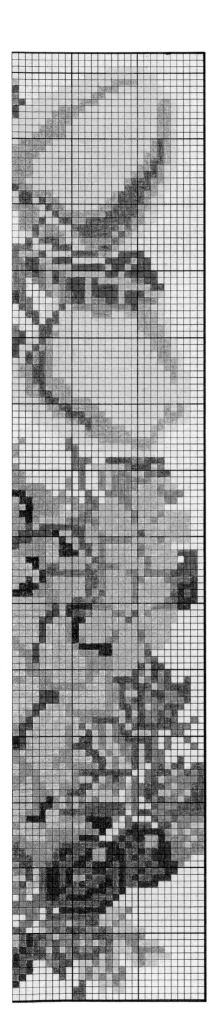

LARGE PINEAPPLE

STITCH COUNT: 143 x 143
FINISHED STITCHED SIZE: APPROXIMATELY 35.5 x 35.5CM (14 x 14IN)

Materials

43.5 x 43.5cm (17 x 17in) #10 mesh canvas (this allows for a 4cm (1¹/₂in)
margin all the way around the design)
No. 18 tapestry needle
It's Polite to Point® Heirloom Quality Needleart Wool in the colours listed below

Colour		1.5M (60IN) LENGTHS REQUIRED	Colour		1.5M (60IN) LENGTHS REQUIRED
GN610	Dark blue green	12	YL030	Medium golden yellow	19
GN630	Medium blue green	9	YL040	Light golden yellow	3
GN650	Light blue green	9	PP110	Dark blue purple	3
GN100	Dark moss green	12	PP130	Medium blue purple	7
GN120	Medium moss green	10	PP220	Medium reddish purple	11
GN140	Light moss green	7	PP440	Light lavender blue	2
GN930	Medium yellow green	4	RD410	Bright pink red	5
GN950	Light yellow green	6	RD440	Medium pink	7
OR420	Bright orange red	2	RD460	Light pink	5
OR440	Medium salmon	5	BR010	Dark brown	2
OR460	Light salmon	4	BR030	Medium brown	3
YL010	Bright gold	12	BL790	Teal blue background	31

Use all three plies at a time. For general stitching instructions and conversions
for other mesh sizes, see Basic Techniques, page 11.

Victorian Paisley

A ROLLER-PRINTED FABRIC (1838) IN WINTERTHUR'S COLLECTION OF ENGLISH PRINTED TEXTILES WAS THE INSPIRATION FOR THE BOOKMARK, PICTURE FRAME AND BRICK COVER. THE BRILLIANT DYES AND THE JUXTAPOSITION OF NATURALISTIC FLOWERS AND SMALL PAISLEY MOTIFS ARE CHARACTERISTIC OF THE VICTORIAN PERIOD.

All designers recycle, combine and adapt motifs. The projects here, for example, are interpreted from an English printed textile that was itself derived from the familiar Indian paisley form. Combined with the geometric stripe pattern, more common in the nineteenth century than today, the motifs of two cultures are skilfully intertwined.

Cloth was a major import into Europe from India, which is why so many English words for fabrics and garments are Indian in origin: shawl, calico, cashmere, chintz, khaki and bandanna. Indian craftsmen developed sophisticated methods of weaving, printing and painting cloth many centuries before Europeans did. With the creation of the Dutch (1597), English (1600) and French (1664) East India Companies, the sophisticated Indian cloths found their way into Europe, where their bright colours and exotic patterns were greatly admired.

During the eighteenth century, to the delight of those who could afford them, fine shawls from India arrived in Europe. An Indian weaver might take up to five years to make one shawl that could cost as much as a London townhouse. By the early 1800s, they had become a fashion necessity of the very wealthy. Although the English had access to them first, through the English East India Company, the craze for these shawls may have been sparked when Napoleon gave one to Josephine, who collected more than sixty.

The original cashmere shawls from which the paisley motif was derived were extraordinary garments and remarkably expensive. Anything as desirable as this was bound to be reproduced in more affordable forms. The popular paisley motif actually gets its name from Paisley, Scotland, where enterprising mill owners of the early nineteenth century began to copy the exquisite Indian shawls. They used mechanical jacquard looms that could weave cloth into a pattern in a fraction of the time it took to weave a shawl by hand. The wraps they produced were handsome and relatively inexpensive. Yet printed paisleys were even cheaper and soon eclipsed both the hand- and machine-woven versions.

By the late 1860s any serving maid could afford a printed shawl for a few shillings. That alone may have prompted her mistress to stop wearing paisley shawls. Then the introduction of the bustle in 1869, a dress accessory that interfered with the drape of the shawl, caused its final demise. An entire industry perished, but not before the characteristic teardrop paisley shape became a common motif used in other textiles. A legacy of original and printed shawls, as well as derivative textiles, survive as cherished heirlooms and museum pieces for our study and interpretation today.

Still popular, the graceful teardrop paisley motif adorns the elegant striped fabric I chose from the Winterthur collections for the following projects. The stripe is a constant in both apparel and home furnishing fabrics. The options for utilizing such a directional pattern are somewhat limited because it must be painstakingly sewn so that the stripes meet. The brick cover, however, lends itself perfectly to the long design elements, as do the bookmark and picture frame.

Making the Bookmark

I stitched the bookmark with embroidery silks and one metallic thread, using two strands of the six-strand silks at once, and one ply of the metallic (which is how it comes). Use the colour names in the chart and refer to the picture to select your own fibres.

Trim the finished needlepoint to about 6mm (¹/₄in) from the outermost rows of stitches. Fold the unstitched canvas under. With small running stitches, attach the needlepoint to the right side of the ribbon, pulling it snugly. I placed mine closer to one end of the ribbon than the other.

You can either hem both ends of the ribbon straight, or mitre one end as I did. For a flat hem, fold about 3mm (¹/₈in) to the wrong side twice, then slipstitch the hem in place. To mitre an end, gently (to avoid a crease) fold the end of the ribbon in half, along the length, right sides together. Stitch diagonally across the end, starting about 1.2cm (¹/₂in) from the end on the outside edge, and finishing at the fold about 3mm (¹/₈in) from the end of the ribbon. Trim the seam to about 3mm (¹/₈in), then turn the point right side out.

Set on its velvet ribbon, the luxurious bookmark (below right) makes the perfect gift, and because it's so small it is an ideal starter project. However, once you've made that, you'll want to go on to make the picture frame (top) and brick cover (centre). Use the covered brick as a bookend, paperweight or doorstop.

99

Making the Picture Frame

I chose colours for the picture frame to suit my photograph, selecting the cloth colour first and then my fibres. I chose rayon fibres and one metallic thread, using one ply of the four-ply rayon at once, and one ply of the metallic (which is how it comes). Then I bought the frame. This doesn't need to be expensive because it will be covered up. I drew my frame on graph paper and then laid out the design inside it to ensure it would be centred attractively.

Trim the finished canvas to 28 x 23cm (11 x 9in), leaving a 2.5cm (1in) border all round the needlework. Cut a 2cm (³/4in) square of blank canvas from each corner, following the Aida threads, but don't trim away the unstitched centre yet. Centre the needlework over the frame and wrap the edges to the back. Secure them on the back with tape, staples or glue, taking care not to get any glue on the needlework. Tuck in the raw edges at the corners diagonally and secure as before.

Now finish the inside edges of the frame. Carefully cut into the centre of the canvas and trim it away, leaving a 1cm (³/8in) border of blank canvas all round the needlepoint. Cut diagonally into the inside corners, stopping at the frame. Gently wrap the top and bottom edges of the canvas to the

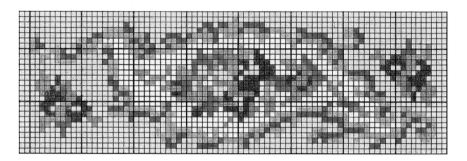

VICTORIAN PAISLEY BOOKMARK

Stitch count: 82 x 26
Finished stitched size:
Approximately 8.5 x 3cm (3³/8 x 1¹/8in)

Materials

*14 x 8cm (5³/8 x 3¹/8in) #24 mesh white congress cloth
(this allows for a 2.5cm (1in) margin all the way
around the design)
No. 26 tapestry needle
50cm (¹/2yd) of 3.2-3.8cm (1¹/4-1¹/2in) wide ribbon
Kreinik #8 fine braid in the colour listed right
Kreinik Silk Mori® in the colours listed right*

For general stitching instructions and conversions for other mesh sizes, see Basic Techniques, page 11.

Colour		10m (11yd) spools of #8 fine braid required
339	Tropical teal/dark blue	1

Colour		5m (5¹/2yd) skeins of silk mori® required
5103	Light blue	1
6106	Dark purple	1
6104	Light lavender	1
3015	Medium rose	1
3013	Light rose	1
4196	Dark teal	1
4193	Medium teal	1
2027	Dark yellow	1
2024	Light yellow	1
8000	Soft white	1

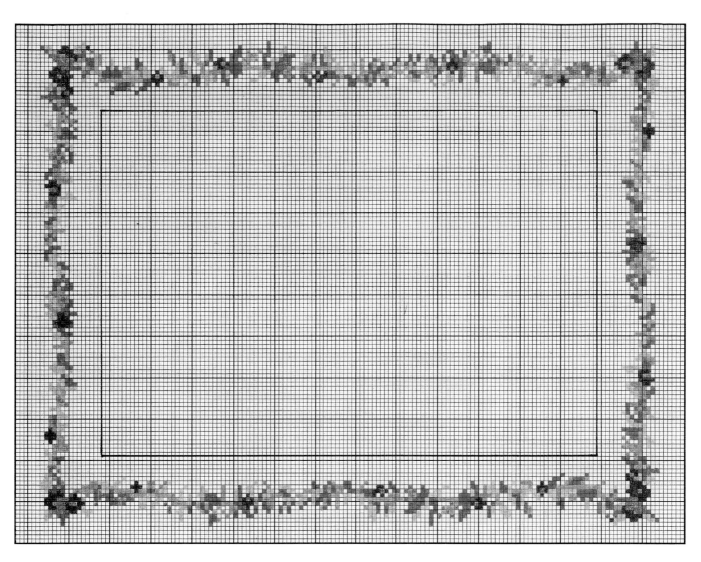

PICTURE FRAME

STITCH COUNT: 163 X 126
FINISHED STITCHED SIZE: APPROXIMATELY
23 X 18CM (9 X 7IN)

Materials

33 x 28cm (13 x 11in) #18 count baby mint (617)
Zweigart® Aida cloth (this allows for a 5cm (2in)
margin all the way around the design)
No. 24 tapestry needle
23 x 18cm (9 x 7in) picture frame with a 3.2cm
(1¹/₄in) border and an inner lip
90cm (1yd) flat trim for outer edges
90cm (1yd) thin cord for inner edges
Madeira Decora rayon in the colours listed right
Kreinik #8 fine braid in the colour listed right

For general stitching instructions and conversions for
other mesh sizes, see Basic Techniques, page 11.

	Colour	5M (5¹/₂YD) SKEINS OF RAYON REQUIRED
	1533 Medium blue	1
	1585 Dark teal	1
	1445 Medium teal	1
	1433 Dark purple	1
	1480 Medium purple	1
	1511 Light purple	1
	1449 Dark green	1
	1447 Light green	1

	Colour	10M (11YD) SPOOLS OF #8 FINE BRAID REQUIRED
	001HL Silver	1

back, and then the side edges, and secure them as before. Try to handle these inside edges as little as possible to minimize fraying. There will be small corner areas not covered by any fabric. Because my frame was a very dark colour, I painted the exposed corners to match the fabric, minimizing them visually, however the cord will also help to cover these areas.

Glue or stitch the flat trim to the outer edge of the frame, joining the ends at the bottom by folding them under and butting the folds together. Apply thin cord to the inside edge of the frame – I tied the ends together in a bow.

Making the Brick Cover

Stitch the needlepoint following the chart. When working on the two short sides, do not turn the canvas and chart sideways. Stitch the entire flat canvas with all the stitches running in the same direction. When the corners are joined, the stitches will run in opposite directions, but on #18 mesh it is not readily apparent. The piece is easier to block and retains its shape better if all the stitches run in the same direction. This advantage outweighs the feature of having the stitches running around the brick in the same direction. See page 121 for details on assembling the brick cover.

BRICK COVER

STITCH COUNT: 224 X 153

FINISHED STITCHED SIZE: APPROXIMATELY 31.5 X 21.3CM

(12³/₈ X 8³/₈IN)

Materials

38 x 28cm (15 x 11in) #18 mesh canvas (this allows for a margin of
just under 4cm (1¹/₂in) all the way around the design)
No. 22 tapestry needle
Mediumweight interlining
Brick or block of wood 19.5 x 9 x 6cm (7⁵/₈ x 3⁵/₈ x 2³/₈in)
19.5 x 9cm (7⁵/₈ x 3⁵/₈in) heavyweight felt
It's Polite to Point® Heirloom Quality Needleart Wool in the colours
listed right

Use one of the three plies at a time. For general stitching instructions and conversions for other mesh sizes, see Basic Techniques, page 11.

	Colour		1.5M (60IN) LENGTHS REQUIRED
	WH210	Charcoal	7
	BL010	Dark blue	1
	BL440	Medium blue	5
	PP110	Dark purple	3
	PP130	Medium purple	3
	PP250	Light rosy lavender	11
	RD010	Burgundy	2
	RD040	Medium pink	1
	RD060	Light pink	2
	GN100	Dark green	3
	GN120	Medium green	4
	BL250	Light green	7
	YL040	Yellow	2
	OR610	Dark burnt orange	2
	BR340	Brown	2
	WH610	Soft white	5

Top

Garden Flowers & Vines

THIS EXQUISITE FLOWERS AND VINES PATTERN WAS ADAPTED FROM AN ELABORATE COLOURED PLATE
FOUND IN A BOOK BY OWEN JONES, WHOSE WORK IS CREDITED WITH INTRODUCING EUROPEANS TO
RARE AND THEN UNFAMILIAR MASTERPIECES OF CHINESE ORNAMENTAL ART.

One of the most visually exciting volumes in the Rare Book Collection at Winterthur is *Examples of Chinese Ornament*. This extraordinarily beautiful book was first published in 1867 in a limited edition of 300 copies that are now among the volumes most sought after by historians world-wide. A significant source for all designers and artists, the book is universally regarded as the classic reference book on Victorian aesthetics, as well as an important visual documentation of the major forms of Chinese decoration.

Compiled and written by Owen Jones, the book contains 100 colour plates showing decorations from painted vases, bowls and other Chinese ornaments. These were objects imported to the West in increasing numbers in the middle of the nineteenth century. The Ti-Ping Rebellion caused the destruction and sacking of many buildings and generated the introduction to Europe of a vast number of magnificent works of Chinese ornamental art. These were of a character rarely seen before by Europeans. The artworks were exceptional, not only for the perfection and skill shown in the technical processes, but also for the outstanding beauty and harmony of the colouring and perfection of the ornamentation.

Owen Jones (1809-1874) was born in London. He was trained as an architect and designer at the Royal Academy and became a teacher of Applied Arts at the South Kensington School of Design. He toured the Middle East (1833) and Spain (1834), researching original designs and illustrating his discoveries. Throughout his life, his theories and colourfully illustrated books exerted profound influence on the evolution and development of decorative arts, especially the design of English carpets, furniture and wallpaper.

Owen Jones' books are valuable and instructive aids in researching the progressive development of design motifs of the past, and they live on – I took my design for the Delft flowers and vines from a picture of a blue-and-white china bottle. For the colourful version I used the palette from a French wallpaper, once again demonstrating that marrying visuals from two cultures in one design can have dramatic appeal. I particularly like this size of design – it is so versatile that you can use it to produce a variety of projects like the ones shown here.

Making the Glasses Case

Follow the chart on page 106 or 107 to make the multi-coloured or Delft version of the design, then block it. Cut the lining to match the needlepoint canvas, then stitch the two together with right sides facing, stitching along the outermost needlepoint stitches and leaving a 13cm (5in) opening along one edge for turning. Clip the seam allowances at the corners diagonally, almost at the seam, and turn the piece right sides out. Slip stitch the opening closed.

Fold the square in half vertically and sew the sides together with a double thread, taking tiny running stitches. Pull tightly so the sides fit together snugly. Stitch the bottom edges together in the same way.

Making the Pocket

I used the needlepoint square to make a bag pocket. Simply line the needlepoint as for the glasses case, then attach it to the bag around the side and lower edges with small running stitches.

Attaching the Box-lid Panel

To mount the needlepoint square on a wicker hamper, first line it as for the glasses case. Attach it to the lid with small running stitches, working down through the lid and back up through the needlepoint. If you catch only the outermost row of stitches and not the lining, the needlework will roll down tightly against the box lid, giving it an almost padded look. Stitch or glue a decorative ribbon trim around the box lid, if desired.

The glasses case (left), bag pocket (centre) and box-lid panel (right) are all made from the same basic versatile design in two colourways. If you prefer, you can frame your finished pieces.

105

MULTI-COLOURED FLOWERS AND VINES

STITCH COUNT: 125 x 127
FINISHED STITCHED SIZE:
APPROXIMATELY 18 x 18CM (7 x 7IN)

Materials

*25.5 x 25.5cm (10 x 10in) #18 mesh canvas (this allows for
a 4cm (1¹/₂in) margin all the way around the design)
No. 22 tapestry needle
23cm (¹/₄yd) lining fabric
It's Polite to Point® Heirloom Quality Needleart Wool
in the colours listed right*

*Use one of the three plies at a time. For general stitching
instructions and conversions for other mesh sizes, see Basic
Techniques, page 11.*

	COLOUR		1.5M (60IN) LENGTHS REQUIRED
	WH210	Charcoal	1
	BR030	Medium brown	2
	BL010	Dark blue	3
	BL040	Medium blue	1
	GN000	Dark green	5
	GN030	Medium green	2
	BL210	Dark teal	3
	YL110	Bright gold	2
	RD410	Red	1
	RD440	Pink	1
	PP130	Medium lavender	2
	WH600	White	13

DELFT FLOWERS & VINES

1.5M (60IN) LENGTHS

STITCH COUNT: 125 X 127

FINISHED STITCHED SIZE:

APPROXIMATELY 18 X 18CM (7 X 7IN)

	COLOUR		REQUIRED
	BL740	Dark blue	12
	BL750	Medium blue	6
	BL050	Light blue	4
	WH610	Soft white	13

Materials

25.5 x 25.5cm (10 x 10in) #18 mesh canvas (this allows for a
4cm (1¹/2in) margin all the way around the design)
No. 22 tapestry needle
23cm (¹/4yd) lining fabric
It's Polite to Point® Heirloom Quality Needleart Wool
in the colours listed right

Use one of the three plies at a time. For general stitch-
ing instructions and conversions for other mesh sizes,
see Basic Techniques, page 11.

Yuletide Greetings

A VARIETY OF COLOURFUL IMAGES FROM BOOKS AND TOY CATALOGUES AND A COLLECTION OF VICTORIAN PAPER ORNAMENTS FROM THE WINTERTHUR LIBRARY INSPIRED THESE YULETIDE PROJECTS. THERE'S A DELIGHTFUL ANGEL STITCHED ON BOTH SIDES THAT CAN SIT ON A TREE OR STAND ON A TABLE AND TWO CAPACIOUS STOCKINGS IN THE SET.

The angel design, shown right, is taken from one of my favourite sections of Winterthur's library, the Joseph Downs Collection of Manuscripts and Printed Ephemera. It is a source of unending inspiration, containing more than 100,000 manuscripts, visual images and printed ephemera relating to American craftsmen and artists, architecture and the decorative arts in America. The fascinating collection includes sketchbooks; drawings; journals; travel accounts and letters; architectural papers; trade catalogues; advertising art; postcards and greeting cards; children's toys, games and paper dolls and much, much more.

Seasonal Inspiration

The Downs collection contains an abundance of angels, especially in an assemblage of Victorian Christmas paper ornaments and cards. The angel project is an interpretation of a paper die-cut ornament, enhanced with a skirt of embossed and gilded paper. These *rauschgold* (gold foil) angels of Nuremburg were the most glorious of the countless Christmas tree ornaments produced in the nineteenth century. Glittering in the reflected light of the Christmas candles, they frequently adorned the top of the tree. These gilded angels were expensive and in limited supply in America. Using paper cut-outs and gold cardboard, ingenious Victorian handcrafters fashioned similar, less expensive versions of these ornaments. The Downs collection also includes many of these imitations.

A paper toy and a trade catalogue in the Downs collection provided the images for the Father Christmas stocking. I interpreted the figure from a nineteenth-century die-cut paper toy. Exquisitely coloured lithographs of the brightly clad figure were also fashionable Victorian decorations. Again, the best examples came from Germany and usually featured the jovial bearer of gifts in a fur-trimmed robe, often blue. The toys completing the design came from a German toy catalogue. Such trade catalogues, produced for both the wholesale and retail markets, focused primarily on products for the domestic environment. The

Based on nineteenth-century toys, Victorian Christmas paper ornaments and a book of children's illustrations, this angel and the two stockings will bring the magic of Christmas past to your festivities.

108

volume I selected, c. 1880-1889, contains hundreds of brilliantly coloured images of German toys.

I returned to Winterthur's Rare Book Collection to obtain images for the companion stocking. Santa's Workshop was adapted from three charming illustrations in *Christmas Pictures by Children,* a book first published in 1922 in Vienna and London. (The Rare Book Collection contains the London edition.) The talented young artists whose pictures were selected for the publication were between the ages of six and sixteen. These children were students of Professor Čižek of Vienna, and their lithographs, done in response to a class assignment, were exhibited in London. The unusual freshness of vision, spontaneity and remarkable ability of the artists are evident in their enchanting illustrations of Christmas fantasies.

The projects portray the images of Christmas that have been a part of our history for thousands of years – these timeless symbols are still popular decorating motifs today. The needlepoint angel will sit on top of a tree or stand up as a table decoration. An alphabet chart accompanies the stockings, allowing you to personalize them with a monogram. Consider adding a few speciality fibres to add some festive sparkle.

Making the Angel

Stitch the angel in standard continental or basketweave stitch, using one of the three plies at a time, but stitch the wings and halo with embroidery cotton (floss), using all six strands. Note that the materials listed with each chart are sufficient to work both sides of the angel, but they are repeated to provide you with a quick reference to the colours in each chart.

Line both sides of the angel separately. Pin the needlepoint and lining together with right sides

This enchanting nineteenth-century paper die-cut angel with a skirt of embossed and gilded paper may once have graced the top of a Victorian Christmas tree.

facing and stitch around the lower edge from the bottom of one wing to the top of the other wing, stitching just along the last row of needlepoint. Round the seam smoothly along the curved areas. Trim the seam allowances to 6mm (¹/₄in), then clip the bottom corners of the skirt diagonally across the seam allowances, close to the stitching. Where the wings join the skirt, clip straight into the seam allowance, almost to the seam.

Turn both the lined angel front, and the back, right sides out, tuck in the remaining seam allowances and slip stitch the openings closed. Pin the two pieces together with right sides out, making sure the pattern matches. Tack (baste) each side where the wings join the skirt and at the tops of the wings to hold the pieces in place. Beginning at one bottom corner of the skirt, hand stitch the two pieces together all the way round with small running stitches, but leave the entire bottom of the skirt open so the angel can sit on a tree.

Making the Stockings

Stitch each stocking following its chart, and adding your initials from the alphabet charts as desired. Block the needlepoint (see Finishing Instructions page 120). Place a piece of tissue paper over the right side of the needlepoint, trace the stocking outline and cut it out to make a pattern. Fold the lining fabric in half and pin the pattern on top. Cut out the stocking through both fabric layers to make a pair, adding 1.5cm (⁵/₈in) all round for seam allowances. Now pin the pattern to the velveteen backing fabric, wrong sides together, and cut out, adding a 1.5cm (⁵/₈in) seam allowance all round.

Pin the two lining pieces together with right sides facing. Stitch around the side and bottom edges, taking a 1.5cm (⁵/₈in) seam allowance and starting and stopping 1.5cm (⁵/₈in) from the top edge. Repeat to stitch the needlepoint to the velveteen, with right sides facing, this time stitching along the very edge of the needlepoint and again leaving the top edge open – start stitching 1.5cm (⁵/₈in) from the top front edge and finish 4cm (1¹/₂in) from the top back edge. Snip into the seam allowances of both the lining and needlepoint at curves for ease and snip off the seam allowances diagonally at the corners. Trim off the excess canvas as necessary.

Turn both sections right sides out to check that they lie flat, and if not, trim or snip the seam allowances a little more. Lightly press the 1.5cm (⁵/₈in) seam allowance at the top of each stocking to the wrong side. Turn the lining inside out again and slip it into the needlepoint stocking so wrong sides are facing. Pin the layers together with the seam allowances on the inside and slip stitch around the top to attach the lining. Leave the small gap at the top of the back seam open.

Finally, attach the trim by hand, starting at the top back of the stocking and finishing by making a hanging loop. Slip the ends of the trim into the gap at the top of the back seam, then sew the opening closed.

This Father Christmas was a nineteenth-century die-cut paper toy and one of my inspirations.

YULETIDE ANGEL
(*Front*)

STITCH COUNT: 183 X 189
FINISHED STITCHED SIZE:
APPROXIMATELY 26 X 26.5CM (10¹/₄ X 10¹/₂IN)

Materials

Two rectangles 34 x 34.5cm (13¹/₄ x 13¹/₂in) #18 mesh
canvas (this allows for a 4cm (1¹/₂in) margin all the
way around the design)
No. 22 tapestry needle
35cm (³/₈yd) lining fabric
DMC stranded embroidery cotton (floss)
in the colours listed right
It's Polite to Point® Heirloom Quality Needleart Wool
in the colours listed right

	COLOUR		8M (8³/₄YD) SKEINS OF DMC COTTON REQUIRED
	729	Gold	4
	780	Golden brown	5

	COLOUR		1.5M (60IN)LENGTHS OF WOOL REQUIRED
	BL540	Light blue	2
	BL500	Dark blue	4
	BL930	Light turquoise	4
	GN650	Light green	2
	YL260	Golden yellow	26
	YL230	Orange gold	3
	YL210	Rust gold	1
	BR150	Dark brown	1
	BL390	Light grey	1
	OR340	Medium salmon pink	1
	OR190	Pale peach	1
	WH610	Soft white	5

Use one of the three plies of wool at a time or all six
strands of embroidery cotton (floss). For general stitching
instructions and conversions for other mesh sizes, see Basic
Techniques, page 11.

Working the Front and Back

The materials above are sufficient to work both the front and
the back of the angel, but they are repeated with each chart so
you have an easy colour reference to follow when working each
side. For details on assembling the angel, see page 110.

YULETIDE ANGEL
(*Back*)

STITCH COUNT: 183 X 189
FINISHED STITCHED SIZE:
APPROXIMATELY 26 X 26.5CM (10¹/4 X 10¹/2IN)

Materials

*Two rectangles 34 x 34.5cm (13¹/4 x 13¹/2in) #18 mesh
canvas (this allows for a 4cm (1¹/2in) margin all the
way around the design)
No. 22 tapestry needle
35cm (³/8yd) lining fabric
DMC stranded embroidery cotton (floss)
in the colours listed right
It's Polite to Point® Heirloom Quality Needleart Wool
in the colours listed right*

	COLOUR		8M (8³/4YD) SKEINS OF DMC COTTON REQUIRED
	729	Gold	4
	780	Golden brown	5

	COLOUR		1.5M (60IN) LENGTHS OF WOOL REQUIRED
	BL540	Light blue	2
	BL500	Dark blue	4
	BL930	Light turquoise	4
	GN650	Light green	2
	YL260	Golden yellow	26
	YL230	Orange gold	3
	YL210	Rust gold	1
	BR150	Dark brown	1
	BL390	Light grey	1
	OR340	Medium salmon pink	1
	OR190	Pale peach	1
	WH610	Soft white	5

*Use one of the three plies of wool at a time or all six
strands of embroidery cotton (floss). For general stitching instructions and conversions for other mesh sizes, see
Basic Techniques, page 11.*

Working the Front and Back

The materials above are sufficient to work both the front and
the back of the angel, but they are repeated with each chart so
you have an easy colour reference to follow when working
each side. For details on assembling the angel, see page 110.

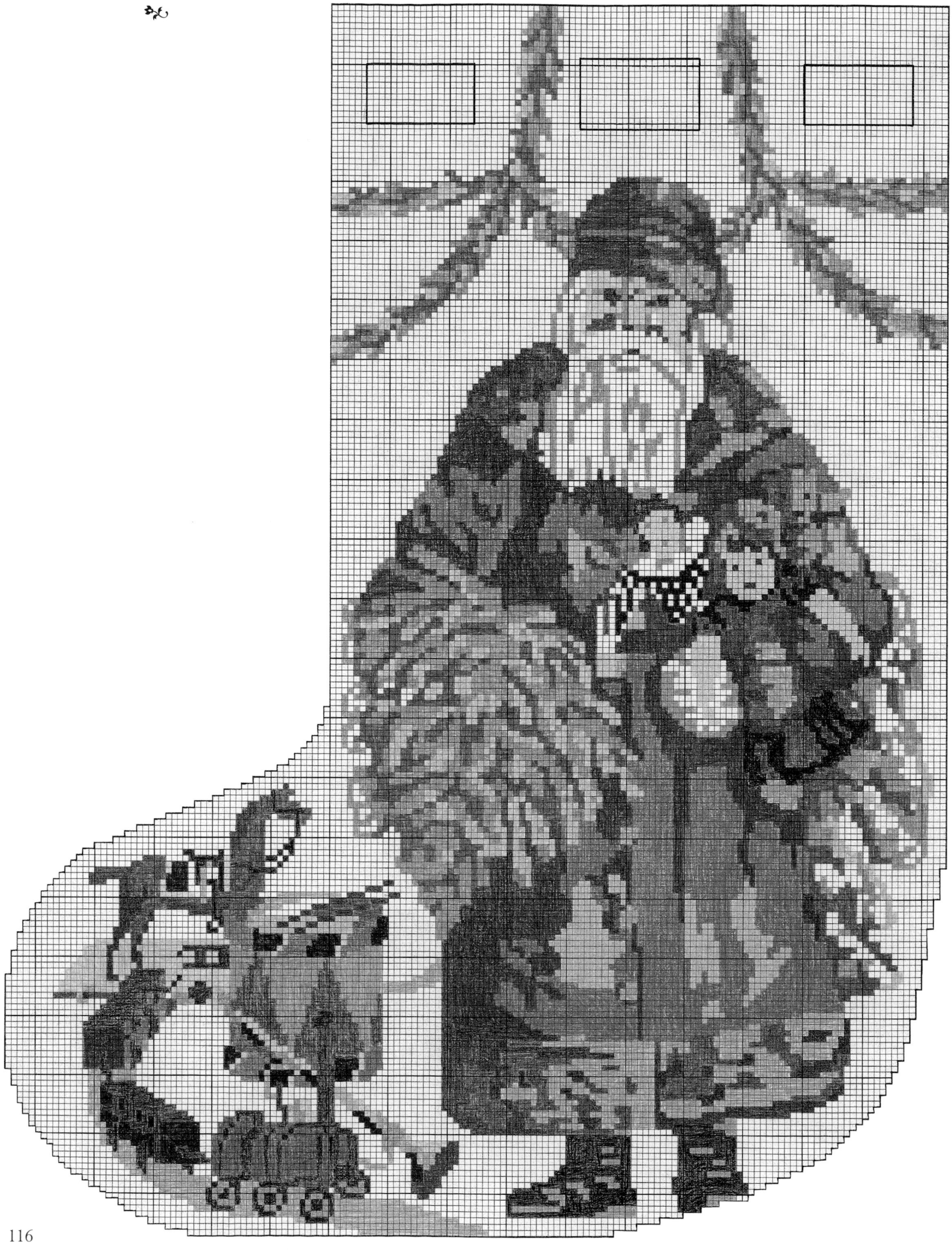

FATHER CHRISTMAS STOCKING

STITCH COUNT: 159 X 207

FINISHED STITCHED SIZE:

APPROXIMATELY 29 X 37CM (11³/8 X 14¹/2IN)

Materials

36.5 x 44.5cm (14³/8 x 17¹/2in) #14 mesh canvas

(this allows for a 4cm (1¹/2in) margin

all the way around the design)

No. 22 tapestry needle

1.4m (1¹/2yd) cord trim

35cm (³/8yd) lining fabric

35cm (³/8yd) velveteen backing fabric

It's Polite to Point® Heirloom Quality Needleart Wool

in the colours listed right

Use two of the three plies at a time. For general stitching instructions and conversions for other mesh sizes, see Basic Techniques, page 11.

Personalising the Stocking

Stitch your initials in the boxes at the top of the design using dark blue wool before filling in the background. You'll find the initials you need below and on page 119. Use this alphabet for the last name initial and place it in the middle box on the Father Christmas Stocking or the centre train car on Santa's Workshop Stocking.

	COLOUR		1.5M (60IN) LENGTHS REQUIRED
	RD500	Dark red	2
	RD540	Medium pink	2
	BL000	Dark blue	13
	BL020	Medium blue	8
	BL040	Light blue	3
	GN100	Dark green	6
	GN120	Medium green	8
	GN140	Light green	5
	WH200	Black	4
	WH020	Grey	3
	BR300	Dark brown	6
	BR320	Medium brown	4
	BR430	Light golden brown	7
	YL120	Yellow	1
	OR190	Light peach	2
	WH610	Soft white	38

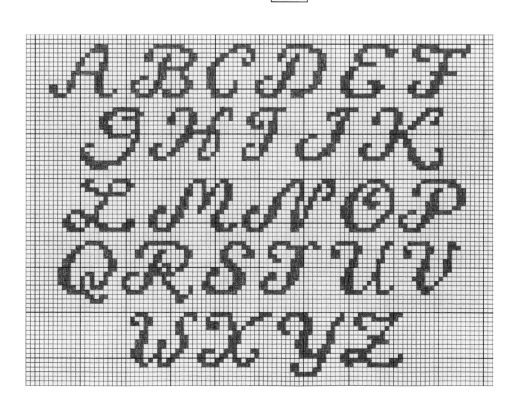

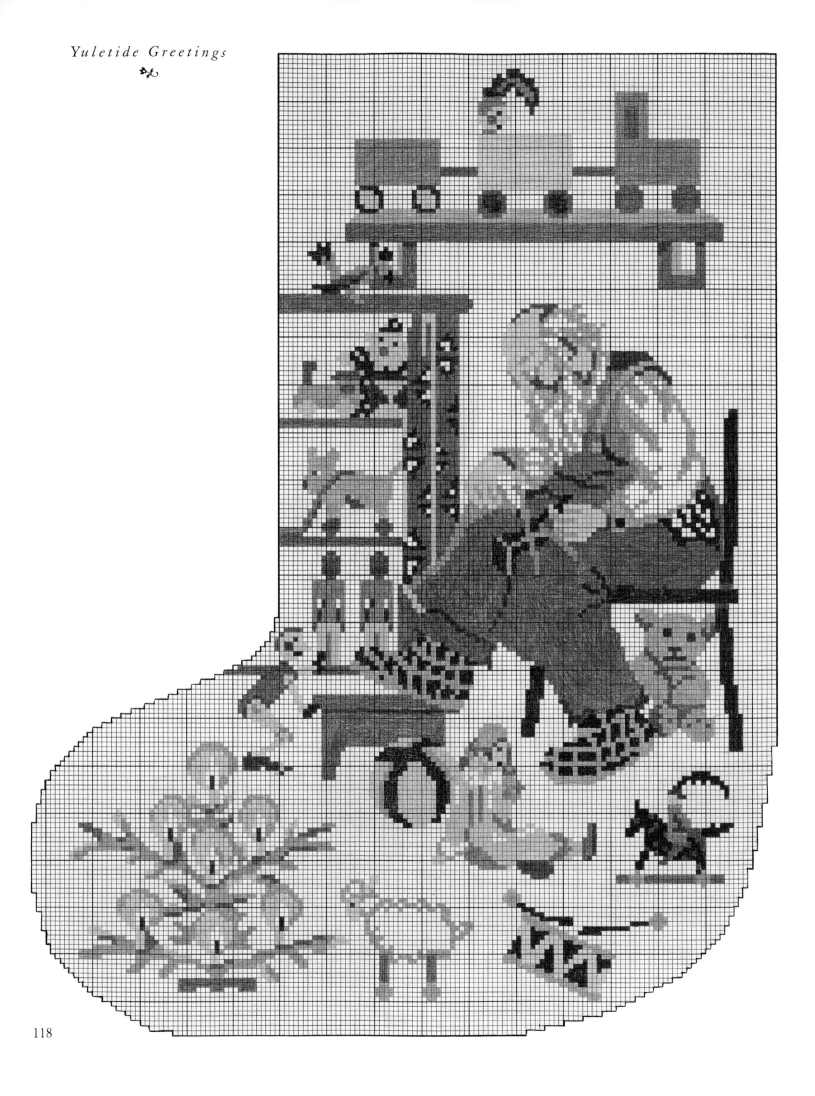

SANTA'S WORKSHOP STOCKING

STITCH COUNT: 159 X 207

FINISHED STITCHED SIZE:

APPROXIMATELY 29 X 37CM (11³/₈ X 14¹/₂IN)

Materials

36.5 x 44.5cm (14³/₈ x 17¹/₂in) #14 mesh canvas

(this allows for a 4cm (1¹/₂in) margin

all the way around the design)

No. 22 tapestry needle

1.4m (1¹/₂yd) of cord trim

35cm (³/₈yd) lining fabric

35cm (³/₈yd) velveteen backing fabric

It's Polite to Point® Heirloom Quality Needleart Wool

in the colours listed right

Use two of the three plies at a time. For general stitch-ing instructions and conversions for other mesh sizes, see Basic Techniques, page 11.

Personalising the Stocking

Stitch your initials on the train carriages at the top of the design in dark blue wool before filling in the rest of the carriages following the chart. You'll find the initials you need below and on page 117. Use this alphabet for the first and middle name initials and place them in the first and last boxes on the Father Christmas Stocking or the first and last train cars on the Santa's Workshop Stocking.

	COLOUR		1.5M (60IN) LENGTHS REQUIRED
■	RD500	Dark red	7
■	RD540	Medium pink	1
■	BL000	Dark blue	3
■	BL020	Medium blue	4
■	BL040	Light blue	2
■	GN100	Dark green	6
■	GN120	Medium green	3
■	GN140	Light green	2
■	WH020	Grey	2
■	BR320	Medium brown	10
■	BR430	Light Golden brown	8
■	YL120	Yellow	3
■	OR190	Light peach	3
□	WH610	Soft white	51

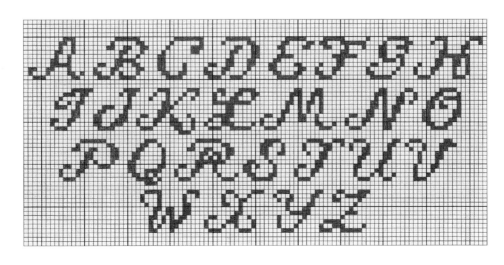

FINISHING TECHNIQUES

Before you prepare your needlepoint for finishing, check that you have completed it properly. Hold it up to the light and look at the right side, making sure it is completely and evenly covered. Then check that all threads are fastened on the wrong side. Also make sure that you have not woven dark threads behind light threads or passed them behind unstitched areas of light-coloured cloth which can create shadows on the front.

Cleaning

If your piece is quite grubby, have it professionally cleaned before blocking it. Tell the cleaner not to press or iron the canvas, as this will flatten the stitches. If the piece is lightly soiled, you can use a mild soap – clear or white soft soap works best. A coloured or perfumed soap may harm the threads with chemicals or tint the dyes. Be sure to obtain information about any threads you have used to determine whether you can wet clean them or not. Use cold water only.

I have actually cleaned greatly soiled pieces myself, after accidents have rendered them filthy. I have soaked entire pieces, even after finishing, in cold, soapy water. Of course, this rinses every bit of sizing from the cloth, but a softer, slightly misshapen cushion is better than an unusable dirty piece. Blot it clean and squeeze out excess moisture with a towel. Never rub the surface or wring the piece, as this can break fibres. Allow to dry naturally for as long as it takes.

Occasionally, I have had a fibre colour run. Usually the piece can be soaked in cold water until the excess dye rinses out. Keep changing the water until it is clear and all the excess dye is rinsed away.

Blocking

Stitching usually pulls the embroidery out of shape. Before the needlework can be made into a finished product, it must be blocked or stretched back into shape. I do this myself, as you can too, or you can have it done professionally. Most needlecraft shops, specialist framers and many upholsterers provide this service.

If the piece is not soiled or misshapen, place it face down on the ironing board and slightly dampen the back with a sprayer or damp cloth. Then place a dry cloth on the back and press until dry.

I usually have to block my needlework. Even when I work in a frame, my piece develops a slight skew. Blocking also helps to even out the stitches. Unless the piece has silk or metal threads it can probably be wet-blocked safely. Blocking can be performed dry for such special threads. Be sure to obtain information about the threads you have selected to know which procedure is best.

SETTING DYES

Heat-set the dyes on wool or cotton fibres before you block the piece. To do this, place the finished embroidery in a dryer on normal heat for about 25 minutes – but check the process is suitable for your fibres by testing it on your scrap canvas first.

WET BLOCKING

To wet-block, dampen a never-bleached, preferably white, cloth or towel with cold water and squeeze out the excess (bleach can affect yarn colours). Place the canvas on the towel and roll it in a jelly roll fashion. Squeeze it gently to moisten the fabric or canvas. Don't soak the fabric or canvas or you will remove the size (sizing) which helps maintain the shape.

Remove the towel and lay the damp needlework on a clean board marked off at 2.5cm (1in) intervals. If you have used the standard tent continental or basketweave stitch, place the piece right side down; for all other stitches place the piece right side up. Stretch the canvas back to its original form and, using the blocking board marks to align the stitched portion of the canvas, secure the fabric to the board by inserting rust-proof tacks or nails through the unstitched areas.

I allow the fabric to dry for at least 24 hours – usually 48 – before removing it. If a piece is very out of shape, do not remove it from the board. Continue to repeat the dampening and drying process until the piece finally relaxes into a flattened, squared piece. Occasionally, I find that placing a few lightweight objects in strategic positions on the needlework will assist in relaxing out the ripples and puckers while the piece is drying.

Finishing

Finishing can be done by you or professionally. You can seek assistance from your local needlework, fabric and upholstery shops. If you finish the piece yourself, especially needlepoint, simply treat it as you would a piece of upholstery fabric. Do not cut the border too close to the stitched areas, as evenweave fabrics tend to fray with wear. Ideally, neaten the raw edges of the piece with machine zigzag stitch or overlocking as further insurance. I leave at least a 1.5cm (5/8in) seam allowance on large pieces and 6mm (1/4in) on very small ones. Allow the same seam allowance on lining and backing fabrics.

Many finishers will stitch into the stitched area of needlepoint by two or more rows. If you aren't finishing the piece yourself, find out how many rows to add around the design before turning in a piece for finishing. If you don't, you may be disappointed that some of your design is gone when you get the piece back. On small items, extra rows of stitches create unwanted bulk, so skip them and use zigzag stitch to neaten the edges.

Finishing styles can range from simple to elaborate. Because I am no seamstress, I chose simple styles for the projects, using trims to make the items look more elaborate. However, there are many ways of finishing your pieces – refer to sewing books for other ideas.

FINISHING MATERIALS

How each project is finished and in what colours are entirely up to individual taste. Selecting suitable materials relies primarily on the mood or visual effect you want to create.

Begin by assessing the display area to determine the appropriate mood. The colours of the fabric and border or trim have a profound effect on this choice. The type of material and style selected for embellishing, such as simple cotton cording versus elaborate rayon tasselled trim, also influences the outcome. Note throughout the book how different trims change the entire style of a piece from country to elegant. The width of a frame also affects the overall result dramatically. The texture, size and lines (delicate or bold) of your design must also be considered when selecting finishing materials.

Because so many factors affect the final outcome of a piece, take your needlepoint with you to the framer or fabric and trim shop. Most of us have had the experience of selecting a trim using small swatches of threads and then discovering that it does not suitably enhance the needlework. As with colour selection, it is always hard to judge materials and trims if you don't see them together, with the needlework, in proper context.

For the backing material, select a colour that complements the needlework. I usually use cotton velveteen, corduroy, firmly woven wool, moiré or damask, suede cloth, linen or lightweight upholstery fabrics. Stay away from silky fabrics (too slippery), knitted fabrics (too stretchy), heavy upholstery fabrics (too thick and heavy), and lightweight dress fabrics (not enough body).

Finishing the Brick Covers

I bake my brick for two hours in a 300° F oven to remove all moisture. After cooling, I wrap the brick in a piece of interlining and tack it with a few stitches. This prevents the rough edges of the brick from catching the backs of your stitches.

Stitch the cover corners together by hand, starting at any corner, using small running stitches and working from the bottom edge to the top. Carefully line up the stitches or fabric threads on each side of the seam. I find it easiest to stitch the seam with the design right side out, making small, tight running stitches just under the edge of the needlepoint stitches.

If a brick cover is made from evenweave fabric, stitch along a straight edge. Trim the side seam allowance to about 6mm (1/4in) and clip the corner off diagonally where the seam meets the top of the brick cover.

Trim the bottom seam allowance to about 1.5cm (5/8in) from the needlework. Press from the wrong side of the needlework, then insert the brick. It should be a tight fit. If not, you may wish to use a little padding to fill it out where necessary.

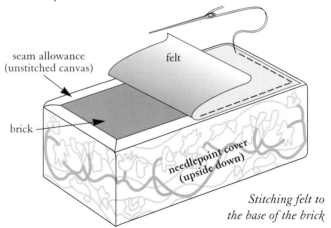

seam allowance (unstitched canvas)

felt

brick

needlepoint cover (upside down)

Stitching felt to the base of the brick

Place the felt against the bottom of the brick, covering the seam allowances on the cover. Use a double thread to attach it with small, tight running stitches (see diagram above).

Lacing

This versatile procedure is used for mounting a variety of projects. Place the needlework face down on a table top. Centre the object – whether a frame, footstool or tray insert – right side down against the wrong side of the stitched piece. Wrap two opposite sides of the needlework back around to the underside of the object, starting with the two longest sides if the piece is rectangular.

Take a length of strong sewing thread sufficient to lace the opposite edges together and begin by anchoring it securely close to the edge of one corner. Stretch this thread across the

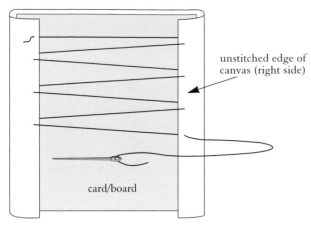

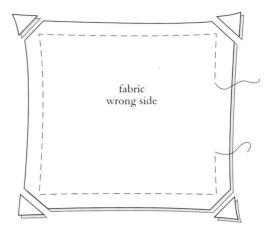

Lacing the finished embroidery

Trimming the corners

back to the opposite edge and catch several canvas threads. Pull the sewing thread quite tight then stretch it across the back to the opposite side and repeat (see diagram above). The gaps between stitches should vary with the size of the project. Use narrow gaps on small projects and longer ones on larger pieces.

Continue this procedure until the edges are securely laced together, almost to the corners. Pull the lacing thread taut so it holds the embroidery in position, then repeat the procedure with the other two edges of the needlepoint.

Do not secure the corners until the end. You will need to experiment with the corners depending on the amount of padding, if any, of the mounting object. On a heavily padded piece, to create the smoothest corner possible, work the fabric into small pleats on the back to reduce bulk. Secure the fabric in place with stitches or staples. For flat pieces, fold the corners back flat, pulling the fold in slightly to be certain that it can't be seen from the front.

Knife-edge Finishing

I use a knife-edge style of finishing for many projects. This simply means joining two pieces with right sides together. Leave an opening along one edge for turning the piece right sides out and, perhaps, inserting a cushion pad. Trim the corners diagonally, almost to the seam (see diagram top right). Turn the piece out, insert a pad, if necessary, and hand-sew the opening closed.

For canvas work, your seam will run between the last row of the design area and the first row of the extra rows that you have added for the seam allowance. If you haven't added any rows, just run the seam along the last row of stitches.

If you choose to make a zip opening in the back, stitch the entire seam closed, all the way around the cover, as the zip is used for turning. I find that the best placement for the zip is

about 5cm (2in) from the bottom edge of the backing. The zip should remain closed while attaching the back, except about the top 2.5cm (1in). This will enable you to reach in and open the zip to turn the cover right sides out.

Attaching Trims

I prefer to purchase pre-made cords, selecting them on emotional criteria, as discussed earlier. If the trim does not have a lip, hand-sew it to your piece at the end. Use a small running stitch along the seam. Open a small hole in the seam, insert the ends and sew the opening closed. If adding a non-lipped trim to a flat surface such as the footstool or picture frame, simply fold the raw ends under and butt-join them with a few stitches. If the trim frays easily, you may need to leave a bit of tape on the raw ends or use Fray Check.

For trims with lips, such as covered piping cord, before adding the backing, pin the lip to the seam allowance of the right side of the needlework, placing the cording along the edge of the needlepoint design. Tack (baste) the trim in place, crossing and securing the ends tightly so that they are smoothly joined together (see diagram below). Then pin and

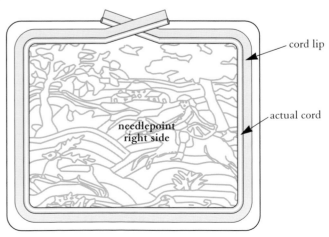

Attaching covered piping cord

stitch on the backing, with the cord to the inside of the seam-line, using a zip foot and crowding the cording. Sew the seam from the wrong side of the needlework in order to follow a row of stitching or a fabric thread for a straight seam.

Adding Fabric Borders

A small piece of needlework can be enlarged and transformed by framing it with fabric or a wide trim. The nap of the fabric for the frame, if any, should always go in one direction. To accomplish this, cut the horizontal frame strips across the fabric and the vertical strips lengthways. The backing piece must be large enough to cover the entire back of the needle-work plus the fabric frame.

To make a bordered cushion front with square corners, first decide which way the borders will overlap. Cut the longer strips the length of the needlework plus twice the border depth and add seam allowances all the way round. Cut the shorter strips just the length of the needlework plus seam allowances. They should all be as wide as the frame selected plus seam allowances.

Sew the shorter strips onto the needlework first, right sides together. Unfold the strips from the front and press the seam open from the wrong side. Then sew the longer strips all the way across the needlework and short strips, right sides together (see diagram below). Finally, attach the back and trim.

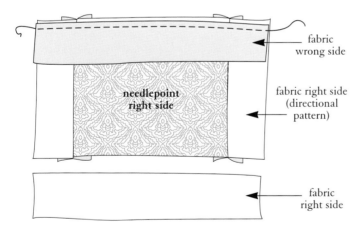

Making a bordered cushion front with square corners

To make a cushion with a mitred fabric frame, cut two strips the length of the needlework plus twice the border width, and two strips the width of the needlework plus twice the border width, adding seam allowances all round each piece. Pin one strip along the appropriate side of the needle-work with right sides facing, matching the centre of the strip with the centre of the needlework side. The ends of the strip should extend equally beyond the needlework edges in

both directions. Sew the strip to the needlework, right sides together. End the seam at the corners of the needlework, leaving the fabric frame corners unattached. Unfold the strip and press the seam before attaching the next strip in the same way

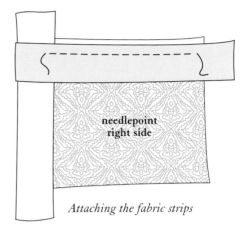

Attaching the fabric strips

(see diagram above). Do not cut the fabric from the corners. With wrong sides up, pull the right sides of adjacent fabric borders together at one corner, aligning them exactly, and pin. Sew a diagonal seam from the corner of the needlework out to the corner of the strips (see diagram below).

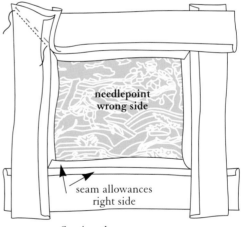

Sewing the corner seams

Trim off the excess fabric at the angle, leaving a 1.3cm (1/2in) seam allowance. Repeat at the other corners. Lightly press open the seam allowances from the wrong side. Then you can attach a trim and backing. You may want to consider a trim around the edge of the needlework, as well as around the outer edge of the fabric frame.

Cushion Pads

To choose the right cushion pad, consider how you will use the cushion and where it will be placed. For a cushion that will receive hard wear, select a sturdy, firmly woven fabric and filling that will keep their shape. You can buy ready-made pads or make your own.

Thread conversion chart

I used my own range of It's Polite to Point® Heirloom Quality Needleart Wool to stitch most of the projects in this book, but you can substitute other fibre brands by referring to the photographs of the projects and the colour names. You can also refer to this chart, but use it only as a guide because it is based upon information supplied by other companies – I have not personally verified the accuracy of the conversions.

Since colour dyeing is not an exact process, dye lots can vary, even within one brand. Always buy enough thread at one time to complete a project, so that the dye lots do not change within your piece. And remember, colour is not an exact science. Colours appear to change depending on the light and the surrounding objects, so never be concerned with getting an exact match to the projects pictured.

ABBREVIATIONS

IPTP It's Polite to Point® Heirloom Quality Needleart Persian Wool

ANCHOR Anchor 6-strand embroidery cotton (floss)

APPLE Appleton tapestry wool

DMC DMC 6-strand embroidery cotton (floss)

PAT Paternayan persian wool

WM Wool Masters persian wool

IPTP	ANCHOR	APPLE	DMC	PAT	WM
BL000	149		336	500	7001
BL010	148	560.8	311	501	7002
BL020	978		322	502	7003
BL030	145		334	503	7004
BL040	140	560.2	3755	504	7005
BL050	159	560.1	827	505	7006
BL130	1033	460.1	932	513	7014
BL150	1031		3753	515	7016
BL200		520.9	3808	520	7021
BL210		520.6		521	7022
BL220	876	520.4	502	522	7023
BL230		520.2		523	7024
BL240		520.1	3813	524	7025
BL250	1042		504	525	7026
BL390					1084
BL410	133	820.3	796	541	7042
BL440	136	460.2	799	544	7045
BL460	975			546	7047
BL500	164		824	550	7051
BL520	161		826	552	7053
BL540	159	560.1	827	554	7055
BL610	121	740.4	793	561	7062
BL640	1033	460.1	932	564	7065
BL730					7101
BL740					7102
BL750					7103
BL790					7133

IPTP	ANCHOR	APPLE	DMC	PAT	WM
BL850			598	585	7086
BL930				593	7094
BL980					7113
BR010		760.7		401	1102
BR030	369			403	1104
BR100		300.5		410	1111
BR120	358	300.3	433	412	1113
BR150					1221
BR220	381	180.7, 580.1	938	422	1123
BR240		980.6		424	1125
BR300	381	180.7, 580.1	938	430	1131
BR310	359	180.6	898	431	1132
BR320		180.5	839	432	1133
BR340		300.2		434	1135
BR350		300.1		435	1136
BR360				436	1137
BR430		900.1		443	1144
BR630		980.5		463	1164
BR650	390	980.8	822	465	1166
BR660					1211
BR750	276	180.1	543	475	1176
BR860	1008	220.1	3773	486	1187
GN000		350.7	520	600	5001
GN010	263	350.6	3362	601	5002
GN030	860	290.2	522	603	5004
GN050	213	350.1		605	5006
GN060					5111
GN080					5113
GN090					5114
GN100		400.5		610	5011
GN110	244		987	611	5012
GN120	243	400.3	988	612	5013
GN130	242	400.1	989	613	5014
GN140			369	614	5015
GN260					5122
GN270	210		562	575	5123

IPTP	ANCHOR	APPLE	DMC	PAT	WM
GN400		340.8		640	5041
GN420	856	250.6, 340.5	3011	642	5043
GN440	842	250.1, 330.2	3013	644	5045
GN570					5142
GN600		290.8	890	660	5061
GN610	218	640.5	319	661	5062
GN630		830.1	3816	663	5064
GN650		640.2		665	5066
GN760					5133
GN930	266	250.2	3347	693	5094
GN940	254		471	694	5095
GN950				695	5096
OR040	311			804	3005
OR190					3094
OR340	328		3341	834	3035
OR350	336	620.1	3824	835	3036
OR410	13	440.8	349	841	3042
OR420	11	440.6	350	842	3043
OR430	10	620.4	351	843	3044
OR440	9		352	844	3045
OR450	8		353	845	3046
OR460				846	3047
OR500		860.6		850	3051
OR530	326		720	853	3054
OR610	340		919	861	3062
OR630				863	3064
OR640	9575	620.2		864	3065
OR700			221	870	3071
OR710	1014, 1015	200.7	355, 3777	871	3072
OR730	1013		3778	873	3074
OR740	868		758	874	3075
OR750	4146			875	3076
PP110	873	450.5	327	311	6012
PP120	97	100.2		312	6013
PP130		880.5		313	6014
PP140	95	880.4		314	6015
PP220		600.4		322	6023
PP250		600.1		325	6026
PP440			3747	344	6045
RD000	897	140.8	902	900	2001
RD010	45	750.8	814	901	2002
RD040			3731	904	2005
RD060	74		3354	906	2007
RD180					2091
RD190					2092

IPTP	ANCHOR	APPLE	DMC	PAT	WM
RD210				921	2022
RD230	894		223	923	2024
RD250		750.1		925	2026
RD260					2101
RD270					2102
RD300		220.5	3721	930	2031
RD310	1024		3328	931	2032
RD320	1023		3712	932	2033
RD330	1022		760	933	2034
RD340	1021		761	934	2035
RD410	39		309	941	2042
RD440		940.3	899	944	2045
RD460	48	940.1	818	946	2047
RD480		870.7		948	2049
RD500	59		326	950	2051
RD510	1025		347	951	2052
RD530	27		893	953	2054
RD540	31		3708	954	2055
WH020	8581	960.3	646	202	1063
WH030	900	960.2	648	203	1064
WH200	403	993.1	310	220	1050
WH210	236	998.1	3799	221	1051
WH600	2	991B.1	white	260	1001
WH610	926	991.1	ecru	261	1005
WH620		992.1		262	1010
WH630				263	1012
YL010	307		783	701	4002
YL030			3821	703	4004
YL040	300		745	704	4005
YL110		840.4		711	4012
YL120				712	4013
YL210	351	470.8	400	721	4022
YL220	1001	470.6	976	722	4023
YL230	1002	470.5	977	723	4024
YL240	307		783	724	4025
YL260	306	470.3	725	726	4027
YL270		470.1	3822	727	4028
YL310		690.6	3829	731	4032
YL330	890		729	733	4034
YL340	891		676	734	4035
YL350			677	735	4036
YL410	374	690.4, 690.5	3045	741	4042
YL420	374	690.4, 690.5	3045	742	4043
YL440		690.2, 690.3	3046	744	4045
YL450	886		3047	745	4046
YL720	290	550.3	973	772	4073

125

Acknowledgements

I would like to express my deepest gratitude to Winterthur Museum, Garden and Library for support throughout the development of this book and design projects, with special thanks to my direct liaisons:

Kristin DeMesse, Catherine Maxwell, Bonnie Maradonna, Ann Coleman, Mary Lew Bergman, Carol Jean Gaumer

Design Assistant: Gail Bolden. **Chartist:** Deborah Prentice-Wright. **Stitchers:** Joan Graham, Marcia Hurst, Linda Litty, Linda Taylor, Elaine Tracy, Lissa Williamson. **Finisher:** Elaine Tracy

Inspiration, encouragement, support and time: *Ruth G. Minor, Lowell C. Minor, Lincoln C. Minor, Donald E. Lamb-Minor*

Suppliers

Look for the following It's Polite to Point® products in fine needlework, museum and gift shops and catalogues: Needlepoint Kits, Printed Canvases and Heirloom Quality Needleart Wool.

In the U.K. a selection of these products are available at:

John Lewis Partnership Department Stores
For the stockist nearest you, contact:

Art Needlework Section
171 Victoria Street
London SW1E 5NN
Tel: (0171) 828 1000

Many U.S. shops carry these products. However, the most extensive selections are available at the following:

Winterthur Shops:
Winterthur Museum Bookstore
Rte. 52, Winterthur, DE 19735
Tel: (302) 888-4741

Winterthur Museum Store
207 King St.
Alexandria, VA 22314
Tel: (703) 684-6092

Smithsonian Shops:
Arts and Industries Museum Shop
900 Jefferson Dr. SW
Washington, DC 20560
Tel: (202) 357-1369

American History Museum Shop
12th & Constitution Ave. NW
Washington, DC 20560
Tel: (202) 357-1527

The Needlewoman East
809-C W Broad St.
Falls Church, VA 22046
Tel: (703) 241-0316

Hook 'n Needle
1869 Post Rd. E
Westport, CT 06880
Tel: (203) 259-5119

Also, view these products on the web at
http://www.hook-n-needle.com

If you have difficulty locating these products, contact:
It's Polite to Point®
1887 Cedar Dr.
Severn, MD 21144-1005 USA
Tel: (800) 688-4424 (U.S. and Canada);
(410) 551-0333 (elsewhere)

You can also use fibres from any other manufacturer that you prefer or that are available. Some other brands I have used are Kreinik, Rainbow Gallery, Madeira, Caron Collection and DMC for speciality multi-fibres; DMC and Anchor for embroidery cotton (floss); Wool Masters, Paternayan and DMC for Persian wool; Appleton and Elsa Williams for tapestry wool and so on. Test all these brands to determine your preferences in terms of quality and budget.

I select my trims and finishing materials from local fabric stores. The miscellaneous products used for finishing, such as the purse, wicker box and picture frame, were all purchased at various local craft stores or speciality boutiques. Look around for other interesting articles on which to mount your needlework.

INDEX

Illustrations in italic